TRINITY LUTHERAN CHURCH
13025 Newell Avenue
P.O. Box 768
Lindstrom, MN 55045

GUIDEPOSTS

Reflections of Heaven

Reflections of Heaven

PETER SHOCKEY

Guideposts®

CARMEL, NEW YORK 10512

www.guidepostsbooks.com

This Guideposts edition is published by special arrangement with Doubleday,
a division of Random House, Inc.

All biblical references are from the *Holy Bible: New International Version*, copyright © 1973, 1978, 1984
by the International Bible Society.
ISBN 0-385-49726-1

www.guidepostsbooks.com
Jacket and interior design by José R. Fonfrias
Jacket photo by Jack Clark/Comstock Images, Inc.
Peter Shockey's photo by Gene Smith
Typeset by Composition Technologies, Inc.
Printed in the United States of America

Dedicated
to my darling daughters
Christina Leigh and Grace Caroline

Contents

Acknowledgments

As I GAZE OUT at our family garden, I am overwhelmed by the beauty and perfection of the living gifts which God has arrayed while inspiring us to create a little corner of paradise on earth . . .

And as I think about the creative projects into which my wife and I are drawn, I am equally overwhelmed by the amazing collection of colorful and delightful people whom God has assembled along our life's path.

I would like to begin by thanking my wife, Stowe, for her faithful reflection of God's love, patience, and encouragement while we walk the path together. I have thoroughly enjoyed this new dimension to our partnership, as she has applied her songwriting talents to the co-authoring of many uplifting stories contained in this book. She gave heart to the writing, and enabled a balance through which it may speak to both mind and spirit.

Also, I am grateful to the authors whose works and interviews inspired the TV programs, and whose generosity in sharing their resources ultimately led to this retrospective book; Joan Wester Anderson, Raymond A. Moody, Dr. George Ritchie, John Ronner, Jodie Berndt, Duane Miller, Ken Gaub, Dr. Bernie Siegel, and Paul Robert Walker.

I am deeply thankful to Pam Kidd, the *Guideposts* contributing writer, for introducing me to so many angels through the stories which she shared. I also appreciate several others at *Guideposts* for their encouragement and guidance along the way; Dick Schneider, John and Elizabeth Sherrill, Lenore Person, and David Morris.

For their devoted help in reviewing this manuscript, I wish to thank Tim Jones, Geralda Shockey, Dick Dailey, Lorrie Eidem, Christine Katcher, and Manon Shockey.

I am eternally grateful to Joe Durepos, my literary agent, whose enthusiasm for this project helped to shape it. He ultimately arranged a perfect match with Doubleday, and specifically with our editor, Trace Murphy. Joe predicted that Trace and I would be a great combination, and he was right! Trace and his colleague, Andrew Corbin, have turned out to be this author's dream team, and I wish to give them a special appreciation. I also want to say thank you to Ann Spangler and Burt Ghezzi for helping me to meet Joe.

There are so many individuals whose names I don't have enough pages to include, but I would like to thank the following for their contributions to my own personal spiritual quest: Mom and Dad, Dick Drehmer and family, Mrs. Seeds, Larry Tomzak and C. J. Mahaney, Dick Runyeon and Alfred Bennett. And those who have been there when the spiritual quest became a creative mission: Victor Rumore, Gene Smith, Wayne Smith, Ron Kristy, Craig Culver, Matt Coale, Blanche Hartner, John Ford, Adelyn Jones, Suzanne Rappold, Ed Emshwiller, Bart Siebrel, Mary Matthews, Robert Bright, Albert Nader, Ladd Allen, Claire Applegate, Mary Francis Fox, Debra Maffett, Lynn Bennett, Jamie Campbell, George Betts, and all at Henninger Elite.

I am ultimately grateful to all of those who shared their stories in these pages—the reader will meet each of them by name—thus giving us all a preview of Heaven on Earth. I appreciate their trust.

Finally, and most importantly, I thank our Heavenly Father for the chance to experience life from *this* side of Heaven; to Christ Jesus for reconnecting us; and to His eternal Spirit of Truth, for keeping us in touch with the Source of creation.

Foreword

SOMETIME DURING THE MID 1990s I had the good fortune to meet Peter
Shockey. I was writing then about angels and miracles, and my books—along
with other authors'—were receiving unexpected attention from the media.
Peter was a documentary film producer, who had been drawn to the same
themes. As I chronicled stories of God's blessings on paper, he was portraying
them on video. But not the trendy, once-over-lightly treatment much of the
television industry was offering at that time, nor stuffy philosophical treatises
that only the most devoted angelologist could comprehend or enjoy.

No, Peter had obviously sensed that such topics were heart- as well as
head-related. His ultimate accounts of what he would call "heavenly visions
for earthly eyes" were outgrowths of his own still-evolving Christian faith,
and involved a willingness to add his questions to the mix. Thus, his films
involved not only visual beauty, but attempts to examine what this sudden
burst of national spirituality was all about.

Is there life after death? How can we be sure? What is a miracle? How do
we know when one happens? How do different faiths regard angels and miracles? Does God seem to be sending more "spiritual signals" now than He for-
merly did? If so, why? What is the point of a miracle? What, if anything,
should happen because of it? Why are the prayers of some people answered,
but (apparently) not others? For me and countless others, his films were
richer for being filtered through the vulnerable eyes of a fellow explorer.

Now Peter presents a book, *Reflections of Heaven*, based on scripts from these
films, adding absorbing details of how and why such stories were selected and
presented. Again, he shares touching moments from his own spiritual mission,

as well as some historical perspectives. But with the passage of a few years, some of the questions have changed: What does this continuing now-world-wide outpouring of spiritual searching mean? Is it connected to the millennium? Is earthly annihilation on the horizon? And what is expected of us, in response to such an amazing time in history?

The key question. From all eternity, it's obvious that God intended to have a relationship of mutual love and trust with the children He created. But evil came, and separated us from the Light. Peter's continuing odyssey, through films and book, has resulted in a conclusion: far from Armageddon being outside ourselves, he believes, the real battle lies within. And each person on earth has a decision to make. Will we remain in the darkness, with its false gods, empty laughter, fear, and anxiety? Or will we choose Light, becoming more intimate with our Father until we realize that the spirit world is the only world that is ultimately real, that the miracles so lovingly documented here have been but brief tastes of the wonders awaiting us?

Reflections of Heaven is a fascinating glimpse of people who have already made that choice, and look forward with confidence to whatever may come. Enjoy it, and prepare to be blessed.

—*Joan Wester Anderson*

# *Introduction*

AS A DOCUMENTARY FILMMAKER investigating reports of supernatural phenomena, I find myself eagerly seeking and catching glimpses of what appears to be the heart of Heaven shining through the cracks of our material world.

An important personal reason lies behind my search. As a young man, I had a spiritual experience that opened my heart to the reality of things unseen—and it left me wanting more. I have been looking ever since for clues to give substance to religious mysteries that are often left as open-ended matters of faith. As bold as it may be to say, *I wanted to find proof of God's existence.* I wanted to find evidence that God is in charge, is listening, and cares . . . As far-fetched as that may sound, though, I am still nonetheless a realist, and when I want to learn about things, I talk with real people who have firsthand experience in those matters. So, when I wanted to explore the reports about angelic beings, miraculous interventions, and the afterlife, I sought out living, breathing people who could tell me what they had witnessed in their own lives. What I discovered was much more than I could have ever imagined, and it has changed my whole way of looking at life.

While exploring the near-death phenomena in the film *Life After Life* with Dr. Raymond Moody, I heard story after story from people who had traveled through a long, dark tunnel into the presence of a bright and compassionate light. The light knew everything about them and loved them, in spite of the wrongs they had done in their lifetime. My memory flashed back to the scriptural references where Jesus said, *"I am the light of the world. Whoever follows me will never walk in darkness, but will have the light of life."* Was this ancient text reflecting what these contemporary testimonies were telling us about the light they had seen after dying?

Sometime later, on the heels of a New York Film Festival award for *Life After Life*, I gained support from Discovery's TLC (The Learning Channel) for more of these investigative documentaries and turned my sights toward *Angel Stories*. This seemed to be a natural sequel, since the near-death experiences included quite a few reports of angelic beings who ushered the deceased into the presence of the larger and brighter light. The subsequent reports we covered in *Angel Stories* were more down to Earth, quite literally, than the near-death experiences because Heaven seemed to be coming *here*, rather than people going *there*. Once again, I felt I was hearing stories that were contemporary, yet were harking back to some very old accounts. If *Life After Life* had shown evidence that God does indeed exist and that we will face Him one day in the afterlife, *Angel Stories* served to convince me that this same God has a well-organized system through which he operates and communicates.

The third film in the series, *Miracles Are Real*, was also a natural offshoot of the previous investigations. While *Angel Stories* had concentrated on angelic appearances and interventions, we had also uncovered many amazing events that were not attributed directly to angels. *Miracles Are Real* was a continuation of this heavenly treasure hunt.

While scripting yet another program, *The Greatest Story Ever Painted: An Illustrated Gospel Account*, I noticed a striking similarity in the historic religious records of the first century and the modern stories that had been reported in the previous shows. And it was not only that the supernatural phenomena rang familiar, but that they appeared as a sudden resurgence after a centuries-long spiritual dry spell at the same eleventh hour before a great historical turning point. Consider this: A civilization built on trust in God becomes rusty with religious hypocrisy and dogmatic structure. It experiences centuries of spiritual decline due to the popularity of Greek-style scientific reasoning. Then, on the brink of a new millennium, bristling with anticipation of a new age of spiritual enlightenment, comes a sudden explosion of fascinating stories of *angels, miracles,* and the *afterlife,* not to mention rumors of an anxiously awaited *final battle* between the forces of light and darkness! This could describe the time of Christ or our own times interchangeably.

By the time I added the historical investigations to the previous contemporary accounts, if anyone had asked my thoughts on the status of the "Kingdom of Heaven," I would have to have said:

> *"Based on the evidence I have heard from so many reasonable people whose lives have been touched personally, I have no alternative but to believe in the existence of a loving Creator. His compassion and intelligence is infinitely superior to our own, and He originates and operates from a wholly different plane than what we can grasp intellectually, namely that of Spirit.*
>
> *"I am also convinced that He has created an organized system for running the universe, in both the physical and spiritual realms.*
>
> *"He has, I believe, provided us with tools and opportunities for communicating with Him and obtaining help and guidance when we need it.*
>
> *"It is not only interesting but vital to recognize patterns in both our spiritual and religious history that seem to be triggered by the millennium swing, particularly surrounding rumors of Armageddon and the end times."*

Finally, I felt compelled to write down this collection of wonderful stories and insights that we have gathered in these television programs. I call this book an *odyssey* because it is really a journey, told in a series of stories. It is my own story, and that of many others. It is the story of one generation's spiritual quest, reflected in the very same quest from generations gone by.

In addition to the stories collected from the shows, you will also read a few stories so profound they couldn't be translated effectively into television. These accounts can finally be done justice by putting them in print, where they can be digested at the reader's own pace.

I hope that you are lifted and illuminated by these stories of people whose eyes sparkle from reflections of Heaven. Perhaps some readers will be brought closer to that ultimate experiment that anyone can do for themselves ... that simple test, in which one calls out to see if God is listening, and then waits for a response. That is the first building block for what we can confidently call *faith*.

—Peter Shockey

PART ONE

Miracles

A Father's Forgiveness

PICKED UP DICK MUSIELAK at the Nashville airport on a Wednesday evening around 7:30 P.M. He had flown in from Houston to be interviewed for the film we were making for TLC (The Learning Channel) on the subject of modern-day miracles. We had dinner that evening in a nice Italian restaurant. I traditionally like to share a meal with people whose stories we will be filming so that we can get to know each other. This allows them to get beyond the first blush of telling what are often some very personal details and gives me a chance to connect with them, eye to eye.

I had first read about Dick's experience in Joan Wester Anderson's book *Where Miracles Happen*, and by the time I met him we had already talked on the phone at length. Still, as we waited for dinner, breathing in the aroma of roast garlic and oregano, I asked Dick if he would go over his story one more time to prepare for our filming the next day.

THE BELOVED SON

It had been a balmy Friday night in Houston, Texas, when twenty-three-year-old Paul Musielak swung into a local convenience store on his way home from a friend's house. He parked in his usual spot and had no sooner gotten out of his car and turned around when—*wham!* From out of nowhere he was broadsided across the head with a blunt object. Repeated bursts of pain to the face and head blurred the image of the two thugs who brutally pummeled him into the pavement. Paul's bloody body was left lying in the parking lot the unfortunate victim of a random attack.

Upon news of his son's attack, Dick Musielak rushed to the hospital to be at his side. As he entered the room and caught sight of Paul, Dick was stopped cold in his tracks.

"I couldn't believe what I saw," Dick recalls. "Paul's eyes were bleeding . . . They were so swollen shut and out of proportion that he looked like some strange creature literally out to here." Dick put a fist to each of his eyes to demonstrate the appalling swelling he had witnessed. "And blood all over his face," he continued. "Paul looked like a piece of raw meat that had just been slaughtered . . . and no one knew yet if his vision would be permanently damaged." He had multiple contusions on his face. Along with a fractured nose and orbital bone, X rays also showed a skull fracture. Doctors suspected that Paul may have suffered brain damage.

Because Paul had received a trauma to the head he was not allowed any pain medication even though he was still conscious. Dick stood by helplessly, watching his precious son suffer in excruciating pain. As endless moments slowly ticked by, one question rolled over and over in his mind: *Who would do this to my boy?* Neither the police nor Paul could offer any clues as to why he had been attacked.

In a daze, Dick left the hospital and headed for home. As he drove, a smoldering anger ignited and began to burn within him. He became obsessed with finding the men who had hurt his son. Not only was he going to catch them, Dick was going to make them *pay* for the pain they had caused. He planned carefully how he would find them and break their kneecaps before turning them over to authorities.

He awoke early Saturday morning, exhausted after a restless night, but more than ready to begin his search for the two hoodlums. He tacked up wanted posters in the neighborhood where the crime had occurred. He talked to people on the street, offering rewards for information leading to the two men's capture. Dick did everything he could think of. But by day's end he still had nothing. Nothing except an all-consuming desire for revenge. This was further heightened by a visit to the hospital to see Paul that afternoon. The doctors reported there had been no improvement in his condition.

Sunday morning found Dick more determined than ever to catch those men. He explains, "I went to church with a baseball bat in my car."

He paid little attention to the sermon. Instead, his mind wandered throughout the service, and he visualized what he would like to do to these horrible thugs.

At some point, though, the minister's powerful words slowly began to seep in. Dick recalls, "Wouldn't you know it, the sermon that day was on *forgiveness!*"

The minister had been quoting Jesus' teachings, "Forgive your enemies and pray for those who mistreat you." Dick braced himself, holding firmly to his anger and almost said out loud, *Not today, Lord.*

But try as he might, Dick could not deny the message that was speaking directly to his heart. The words seemed to be aimed especially at him that morning, "—And when you stand praying, if you hold anything against anyone, forgive him, so that your Father in Heaven may forgive you of your sins." Dick stopped for a moment. He closed his eyes. And as he did, the realization came that he could no longer pursue his vindictive behavior toward those men. He had to forgive them. Somewhere deep inside he knew that he could not ask God for his son's healing if he held bitterness toward the attackers.

And so he began to silently pray, *Oh, God, help me. Help me to forgive those people, whoever they are. Please take these awful feelings from my heart*... Alone in his pew, Dick Musielak sensed a wave of peace overcome him. And there was a tangible shift in his emotional state. Something in his heart was breaking loose, as if a curse had been lifted. And as he forgave the misguided men, tears of compassion welled up as he focused on new prayers for his son. He wept for his son, for the attackers, and at the Lord's ability to forgive.

After church Dick drove to the hospital to visit with Paul. As he exited the elevator, one of the nurses spotted him and said, "Mr. Musielak, it's your son, we don't know how to explain it . . ." Fearing something awful had happened, Dick immediately raced past her and down the hall to Paul's room. He was totally unprepared for the scene that awaited him as he entered.

There was Paul, sitting up in bed! Dick recollects, "The swelling had gone down and he had opened his eyes. That, in and of itself was a miracle." His eyes were only slightly bloodshot and there were no scars, scabs, or bruising. Nothing remained to indicate that he had been severely beaten just *two* days earlier. New X rays showed no sign of a fracture.

Astonished, he asked, "How can this be?"

No one in the hospital had an answer for him. The doctors just shook their heads in amazement.

On Monday Dick and his wife went back to the hospital to check the doctor's exit report for Paul. There it was in black and white. On Saturday's X ray was the evidence of a fractured skull and brain damage. On Monday there was no trace of any fracture at all. Whereas only two days earlier Paul had been treated for deep lacerations and was given the prognosis of certain disfigurement and possibly permanent blindness, he left the hospital as free of blemish as if nothing had ever happened.

❧

As I paid our check and prepared to take Dick to his hotel, I puzzled over his amazing story. I asked myself, *What kind of power had been released by the act of forgiveness in this miraculous healing?* And not only the healing of the son's physical injuries, but of the even deeper ill that had been brewing in the heart of the father? This was just one of many questions we would need to address in the film *Stories of Miracles,* which we were producing for The Learning Channel.

Over the next several months, I would hear many other amazing stories. Little did I know, at the time, that the miraculous memories told by so many people would be transporting me back to my own earliest recollections, and then to a time long before that . . .

CHAPTER 2

A Personal Quest

STOOD ON THE SIDEWALK at 7700 Wisconsin Avenue in Bethesda, Maryland, looking up at the impressive high-rise offices of Discovery Communications Inc., home of The Learning Channel. As I gathered my thoughts for the meeting I was about to have with the VP of Programming, my memory shot back to thirty years earlier, when as a child I had eaten fried chicken at the Top's restaurant located on the very spot now occupied by Discovery. Although I had moved to Tennessee as a young adult and still live there, I had grown up in Bethesda and found it ironic that life would return me to visit the place where my journey had begun so long ago.

For me, Bethesda has always been a meeting place of sharp contrasts, where warmth and open-mindedness clashed with cold and stark materialism. That perception began almost as early as I could remember.

Actually, my first conscious memories go back to my fifth year of life, happily swimming in the sunshine of 1960s Los Angeles, a superficial lifestyle right out of TV commercials of the day. Swimming pools and A-bomb shelters. *The Twilight Zone* and *The Flintstones*.

Four years earlier, when I was one year old, my parents' romantic spirit had catapulted them out of New York City in search of a less chilly emotional climate in which to raise a family. Taking the scenic route, we lived in an adobe house in Santa Fe for a year, a downtown flat in San Francisco for a couple of years, and finally a new suburban rancher with a swimming pool in Glendora, outside of L.A. Dad had landed a great job at Ampex, which had just released a new product called videotape. Within another year a big merger resulted in a management sweep (which foreshadowed the corporate trends of the high-tech nineties) and we were instantly ejected from the great job, house, pool, and *Leave-It-to-Beaver* lifestyle—with the speed of a channel switch.

Waking up on the poor side of town, in a tiny apartment in Santa Monica, I was immediately befriended or rather taken in by a tough boy who introduced me to stealing cigarettes from the sports bags of tennis players at the park, then smoking and gagging behind the bushes. I became as mean as necessary to fit in, once rubbing a sliced lemon onto the skinned knee of a younger neighbor girl, just to watch her cry. At seven years old, I was already headed for whatever the street life of a poor kid in L.A. might lead to. And then the channel switched again.

Dad was offered a job by a former co-worker who was currently working at the IRS in Washington, D.C. The federal government position was just what our family—Dad, Mom, my sister, Christine, and I—needed in order to restart life in the security and safety of a nice old house in suburban Bethesda, Maryland. It turned out to be the long-range opportunity my father had hoped for, and he continued to be promoted until his comfortable retirement fifteen years later.

The move for me, however, was quite traumatic, and I didn't cope very well.

"Everything is so overgrown," was my first reaction to seeing the abundant trees and vegetation that had been so sparse in California. "And everyone seems so unfriendly."

It was a completely different climate, both physically and emotionally, and the East Coast chill that my parents had escaped by leaving New York had crept back into this season of our lives. I didn't fit in very well with the kids who had been hazed in this traditional, materialistic, and politically minded school of thought. Children in this new place had learned at a very early age to be two-faced. One of my first neighborhood friends destroyed me one day during recess at Bethesda Elementary School by ridiculing me with obscenities in front of all the other children. I thought we had been best friends. In California I understood what a friend was, and I understood what it was to be mean. But I didn't understand the rules to these strange games—sarcasm, scoffing, "in-crowds" and social climbing—and I wanted no part of them. So I withdrew.

After school I would run home to avoid being taunted, and then sit in front of television eating buttered cinnamon toast to comfort myself. Between second and third grade I put on twenty-five pounds, which immediately gave the critics something more to tease me about. My parents were concerned by my isolation and urged me to join the neighborhood softball team, the Edgemoor Tigers. I have memories of tripping over myself during one of my few base runs, and skidding on my face to the jeers of my teammates. At the team Christmas party, someone announced that a special treat had been provided for me—a can of Metrical diet drink. My self-esteem was at an all-time low and I had no way to escape the hard reality that surrounded me.

I am now aware that I did what people often do when they are attacked and made to be fearful. I became that which I feared. I resorted to taunting my little sister, and we fought like we never had before. I am told that when

Christine was born several years earlier in California, I had been very protective and loving toward her. But now I was treating her the way I was being treated by my peers. It must have been obvious to my parents what was happening to me, because my father said something one day that still echoes in my mind like a gong. He said, "I don't know what's gotten into you, son . . . you used to be such a nice little guy to have around." To say I was frustrated would be an understatement. I protested to him in the silence of my mind, *Well, you never should have brought me here,* and *Why can't we move back to where the people are nice and the pollen doesn't make me wheeze!* But of course we stayed, and I adapted in order to survive the storm of my developing psyche.

I discovered quite early that creative pursuits had their rewards. Instead of playing kickball with the boys, I would sit in the "tunnels"—concrete pipes fashioned into playground equipment—and would make sculptures out of the playground's muddy clay, to the great admiration of girls whose attention I couldn't get by playing sports.

My mother, an art teacher at a local private school, provided a safe haven for me to further develop my creative inclinations. She devoted our entire garage to set up an arts & crafts studio, open to all the neighborhood children, and I gained a reputation for being an experimenter of various optics, illusions, and gadgets, which gave me alternative ways to develop childhood self-esteem.

By seventh grade, I had regained control of my waistline by a sheer act of willpower and began exploring life's horizon for other things that I could do with my life. I went with a friend to see 2001: *A Space Odyssey* and was absolutely captivated by the visual effects and by the transcendental nature of the story (I have seen the film over twenty times in my lifetime, and probably a third of those viewings were during its initial release). I knew right then and there that I wanted to make films, and that an exciting future lay ahead of me.

As to religion, I can't say I had much exposure or for that matter even the slightest interest. I was told we were Presbyterians. I was also told we were Republicans. So, my only practical use for the information was as a conversation starter: "What religion are you?" and "Are you a Republican or a Democrat?" to which I distinctly remember the mother of a new friend replying, "It doesn't matter what religion we are, and besides it isn't any of your business." So, with the exception of going to the Bethesda Presbyterian Church religiously—on Christmas and Easter—there wasn't much education or indoctrination. I'm grateful to my parents for being honest enough to not be hypocritical about the subject, as it allowed me to pursue my own interests at my own pace without being turned off to the emptiness of religion without spiritual substance.

There actually was one kernel of sincere religious nourishment that came through a devout woman, aptly named Mrs. Seeds, who lived four doors down and who opened her home once a week during the summertime for a children's Bible study. I know I went mainly for the refreshments she served afterward, but I was forever impressed with the memory of the saintly woman who took care of her wheelchair-bound husband and seemed to think a lot of a Bible character named Jesus.

Grade school through junior high was spent struggling with the same things that most people of that generation dealt with. We had to wear the right shirts—paisley, polka dots, or striped; the right pants—wide-wale corduroy, then denim, bell-bottoms, then hip-huggers; and the right shoes—Hush Puppies, penny loafers, clodhoppers, and ultimately hippie boots. It was pretty important to be "different" in the same way as everyone else.

Admittedly, I had learned to conform to the logic of my surroundings in order to survive. Wearing the right things, saying the right things, listening to the right music, and so on. Although I didn't strive to be part of the in-crowd, I strove at least to be part of my own generation. And there was one attribute that I can proudly credit to the peer group with whom I came of age, the teenagers of the mid to late 1960s: We were and forever will be remembered as the generation that seriously questioned the status quo and aspired to find—often crashing and burning in the process—one's own personal journey to discover the true *meaning of life.*

I wasn't consciously looking for anything spiritual, but I was searching for myself, as most teenagers do. I had become aware of my own sarcastic attitudes, and often didn't like the things I heard coming out of my own mouth, knowing fully well that sarcasm from others could still cut me to the heart. I saw that I was developing into the very kind of iceberg that I had run into as an innocent child when we had moved East. I didn't like what I was becoming, but the only alternative was being stepped on and abused, and I wasn't going to stand for that.

A class bully named Randolph had been picking on me for several weeks, taunting and shoving me and generally haunting my dreams. He wore a sickly sweet cologne that smelled like honey, and I can still remember the knots in my stomach when I caught that whiff in the hallway. One day he cornered me alone on the front steps and began tormenting. I just exploded and thrashed him with a fury that surprised both of us. Of course, he was forever pleasant to me after that, but I had seen a part of myself that shocked me. I had wanted to kill him, and it frightened me.

I had learned to cope with the callous world by building calluses. Survival of the fittest meant a toughened ego, and I had learned to never let my guard down.

That may be the reason I was drawn into a friendship with a fellow ninth-grader named Tim Drehmer. Tim had just moved to town from Atlanta, and had learned even faster than I how to build up his defensive wall. He took on a tough guy named Jeff and tempered him in no time. Tim was strong, good-looking, and had an early crop of whiskers, so he had a confidence with girls that I wanted to learn. We hung out after school and I would listen to him practice guitar.

Tim was one of two other guys with whom I started to make movies. Our first project was a documentary for a history class reenacting the Boston Tea Party. Tim, Reed Sturtevant, and I made a good filmmaking team, and we made nearly a dozen independent films before graduating from high school. Tim usually was in the starring role, Reed researched interesting techniques (he would graduate early, and go on to MIT, becoming one of the early program developers at Lotus), and I would usually come up with the story ideas and then direct the movies.

That summer, in the August between ninth and tenth grade, Tim invited me to join him and some of his church friends on a beach retreat in Rehoboth, Delaware. Tim's father was the associate pastor of the Chevy Chase Baptist Church, and was in charge of the small youth group of about twelve kids ranging in age from around thirteen to eighteen years old. Tim and I were fourteen at the time, and he had a budding romance with a thirteen-year-old girl named Cathy, who would also be attending the retreat.

I didn't know what to expect from a retreat, but it sounded like a good vacation, so I agreed to go. After settling into our rooms at the summer cottage that the church had rented and then taking a dip in the ocean, Pastor Dick Drehmer gathered us together for our first of several meetings we would have that week. In his opening prayer, I recall Mr. Drehmer praying in a way that I had never heard before. It was conversational—maybe even ad-libbed—and not at all like the recited prayers I had heard on my infrequent holiday visits to church.

We then began what in those days was called a "sensitivity session," followed by a rap session (remember when rapping was a conversation and not spoken lyrics?). During the sensitivity session, we did trust-building exercises in which, for example, we would all encircle one person who would rigidly lean onto the group's ready hands and then be passed around in the collective trust of our mutual support. Other exercises involved drawing symbolic pictures of how we felt about our ability to connect with other people, or with God. I drew myself climbing over a wall that kept me from seeing the beautiful sunrise on the other side.

To my surprise, most of the other kids in the group had similar feelings of being somehow blocked off from the ability to share love or compassion. Mr. Drehmer was quick to pick up on the term "sarcasm," which several of us used to describe the defensiveness we had developed in order to survive in an unfriendly environment. Then he quoted one of Jesus' teachings about "Doing unto others as you would have them do unto you," and it seemed to hit a bull's-eye. We all agreed that the sarcastic joking that we used on other people tended to hurt our own feelings when used on us.

We heard many of Jesus' teachings during those few days, taking turns reading them aloud. I was moved by the surprising revelation that Christ's number one priority, the first and Greatest Commandment, was to love God with all your heart, soul, mind and strength; and the second, similar to the first, was to love your neighbor as yourself!

Jesus really knew how to sum up life's priorities, I thought to myself. Inside I knew that anyone who was so perceptive about God and about human nature must have truly grasped the meaning of life.

Then we read a statement of Jesus' that baffled me as something unbelievable and even absurd. Tim's father asked me to read another of Jesus' teachings out loud: "Behold, I stand at the door of your heart and knock. To anyone who opens I will come in and dine with him, and he with me . . ."

"But how can that be?" I blurted out. Although I didn't want to step on anyone's religious beliefs, this seemed like a ridiculous statement coming from a man who had been dead for nearly two thousand years. I had been quite ready to buy Jesus' teaching about love and compassion, but this other material was borderline crazy, even spooky.

Later that evening, by the soft glow of the porch light, I picked up the conversation again with Tim, Cathy, and another girl named Karen. Although none of us knew much more about Jesus than what we had just read, our curiosity was quickened. Tim had the most exposure to religious doctrine but was ready to admit that he didn't have answers to all the questions that had been raised.

It occurred to me that if there was any truth whatsoever to the invitation that Jesus had given about *opening the door of our hearts*, then perhaps He could answer some of the unresolved issues that were puzzling us.

So, as an open-minded experiment that would either yield some trace of evidence of Christ's eternal Spirit or else put the idea to rest forever, the four of us joined in a simple and awkwardly stammered prayer. Hands joined, eyes closed, and heads lowered, we talked to someone "out there" who had been dead and gone for nearly two millennia.

What happened next has been forever engraved in my heart, mind, and memory. In the silence of our waiting for an answer, I heard a murmur. It began like the sound of a child's soft cry—a choked-off sob of emotion trying to come out from the depths of a tightened throat. It was coming from inside of me. And then I felt something stirring from deep within. I can still only describe it as the sensation of a bird trying to take wing from inside of my chest, in the area of the solar plexus. And something else . . . Someone had entered the room—I could tell, I could feel it! Someone's powerfully electrical presence was there with us—and *I knew who it had to be* . . .

My eyes fluttered open, but they were filled with tears, making patterns of lights swirl and then settle into focus as I glanced around to get my bearings and see if my friends were aware of what I sensed was happening. We were still holding hands, and I could see that my friends were choking back tears also. A surprised laugh burst from me, upon seeing that they had also been touched by this mysteriously divine presence. As they each opened their eyes, I could see their faces were radiant! They had a "look" that I have since recognized in babies and people in love: dilated pupils and a grin that comes from deep within.

I didn't have to ask if the others were experiencing the same deep spiritual awakening, or whatever you want to call it, that I was. But we slowly and delicately, as if in the presence of a visiting butterfly that we didn't want to disturb, began to talk about what was happening.

I don't have enough pages to describe the love, wisdom, and insight that coursed through the four of us for the next several hours as we took turns carefully listening to one another. We knew that we were being spoken to, and spoken *through*. Egos were lovingly subdued in order to give attention to Spirit.

This experience became *the defining moment* in my life, the turning point that would forever affect my decisions about friendships, romances, career . . . everything that was to come. But the force of change was not only from the spiritual connection that had occurred. I was about to discover an enormous chasm that had opened before me as a result.

The four of us decided that we couldn't keep our excitement to ourselves any longer. We raced down to the beach to share our joyful discovery with our friends, who were playing football. We grabbed their ball and buried it in the sand, urging them to gather around and listen as we enthusiastically tried to explain what had happened. We stumbled through the retelling of our prayer, and the explosive feeling of love, and knowing that Jesus had just now entered our hearts. It sounded somehow trite and unconvincing, even to me, as we listened to ourselves struggle for words to describe the phenomenon we had experienced.

Blank stares. Nervous chuckling. Distant nodding.

Finally someone replied, "Great . . . where's that football?"

I was stunned. I couldn't believe the response. Were we speaking Latin? Here we were, sharing the most amazing thing that could ever be, wishing only to share the greatest love in the universe, and we were virtually rebuffed. It made me angry, and then it was all over. That great sense of loving connection with all living things had vanished! It was as if a great cosmic circuit breaker had blown, and that electromagnetic force that had held us aloft for hours suddenly disappeared, crashing us with a thud to the sand.

I had immediately stepped into the same hole that religious people have been trapped by since time immemorial. We were trying to present a spiritual phenomenon through logical words, which is like trying to share a fragrance with someone with a cold, or music with a deaf person. We had experienced an aspect of life using a sense that had just that moment been turned on. Trying to share Christ's invitation with anyone else would mean first convincing them to willingly let their spiritual perception be activated. And that would require a conscious lowering of their ego, by their own choosing. But you simply cannot force a defense barrier to be lowered: Isn't that the very purpose and mission of the ego, to defend and protect itself from powerful outside forces? The predicament was perfectly clear, as were the horrible consequences of where we might be heading. Religious crusades have slaughtered millions in the name of love, forcing people to accept Christ to avoid the fires of Hell.

Still, this *Light*—this *Love*—beckons to share itself with others. But I understood that logic and intellect would not be sufficient to go where this quest might be leading. How does one share this spiritual beacon, this *light* who exists in a dimension that transcends time and space? Words are not enough. How can one convey the earthshaking implications that this light may be linked to the very source of life itself? That humanity's search for ultimate love and reconnection to God might be found inside one's heart? As Jesus said, "The Kingdom of God is within you!" And how does one communicate all this without using threadbare religious jargon?

I didn't realize it then, but answering such a challenge requires one's entire life and the commitment of every ounce of energy and available resource one can muster. And that is only the beginning. It requires the collective experiences and testimonies, talents and skills, faith and courage from hundreds of fellow travelers that one meets along the way. And even the sum total of all those human efforts, by itself, amounts to no more than a whisper in the wind. Presenting God's love to a frozen world takes all the creative energy, wisdom, and resourcefulness in the universe. It takes the powerful infusion of spiritual Light into the darkness of human affairs, and then the day by day guidance of that loving Light. In other words, it takes a miracle.

❧

As I sat in the sixth-floor office at TLC, pitching an idea for another show on divine encounters in today's world, I looked out the window and could see children on the playground of my former school in the town I had once called home. And it gave me an unexplainable feeling of connection.

CHAPTER 3

The Millennial Quest

VER THE TWENTY-FIVE YEARS that followed my experience at the beach retreat, I have come to realize that my personal quest is actually a reflection of a much larger quest of my generation, which is leading humanity into our children's world of the next millennium.

My contemporaries, coming into their own during the 1960s, were a generation of seekers. Young people who were disillusioned by the materialistic and seemingly brutal world they were inheriting sought alternatives to what they saw as the sins of their parents. The "Love Generation" made a permanent and decisive impact on civilization, although their idealism was often mixed with youthful hormones, creating strange brews that confused free love with free sex, pacifism with violent protest, and spirituality with drug-induced revelations. Then, as unavoidably as getting wrinkles, my generation eventually became parents, facing the hard realities of survival that humanity has faced for countless ages. Many grew up to embrace the materialistic, competitive, and carnivorous attitudes they had previously despised.

But the resounding call for love, peace, and harmony began a domino effect in society that can still be felt. The environmental movement has led to a generation of recyclers and genetic engineers who seek to develop fast-growing timber forests, among other things, and are written up in *Time* magazine as *Heroes of the Planet*. The Far-Eastern-vegetarian-yoga-guru movements endorsed by the Beatles have matured into whole industries encompassing healthful diets, fitness, and countless publications and media serving what is now called mind-body-spirit demographics. Perhaps one of the most remarkable conclusions of that idealistic quest for love, peace, and life's true meaning was its effect on religion and spirituality in the end of the twentieth century. Western society is currently experiencing one of the biggest popular revivals in spiritual interests since science and religion parted company centuries ago at the birth of the age of scientific reasoning. Public opinion polls like Gallup, *Time*, and CNN confirm that a vast majority of people engage in prayer regularly. And just as surprisingly, the interest in things like prayer, angels, miracles, and the afterlife has seemingly sprung spontaneously from *outside* of efforts of major organized religions.

I have several thoughts on why those trends have developed and where they are leading our collective spiritual awareness. But I would first like to continue sharing my own personal journey, and how it led into a unique career path, which I regard as *tracing threads in the fabric* of our shared awakening.

∽

In the days following my profound beach retreat encounter, one question kept coming back: *What had happened to me?* I knew it was far more than just an emotional experience, although it was highly charged with emotion. It was much deeper and more permanent. It could only be described as a *spiritual* experience. But I had no earthly idea what that meant and I wanted with all my heart to find out more. So I began a search for answers to my questions which brought me very naturally into two areas of investigation: *Biblical insights* and *real-life experiences.*

Examining Scriptures lead me to join various Christian groups, prayer meetings, fellowships, worship services, and Bible studies, which seemed to be the obvious sources of insight into Jesus' teachings. Through time, I came to discover many profound truths in the life and teachings of the one who had been called the *Christ, Messiah,* and *Anointed One.* He had revealed to people—through twenty centuries of lifetimes that now includes mine—a radical new outlook on human behavior, spirituality, and the eternal Kingdom of God. It was as revolutionary then as it is today.

It didn't take long, however, before I realized that the emphasis in some churches was on behavioral codes of do's and don'ts and closely parsed religious doctrines instead of the vital spiritual force one reads about in the Gospel. Ironically, it seemed that many Christian groups were filling the very role of the dogmatic "keepers of the law" that Jesus had such conflicts with. When Jesus referred to being "born again," I know he was speaking about an awakening into another realm, which is an intimately personal experience. But frequently I heard the term being *born again,* and *saved* as amounting to a poke-in-the-ribs response to an altar call in order to qualify for Heaven and avoid the fires of Hell. The risk of this definition can be a religious membership rather than a relationship with a living God.

I don't question the sincerity of those who have been introduced to God through a traditional religious upbringing. I know that a genuine relationship can grow slowly and quietly by professing one's faith publicly, through baptism, for example. But Jesus did say that one needed to be born of the *water and of spirit,* in order to see the Kingdom of God. I also don't mean to accuse any particular churches, organizations, or denominations of being hypocritical, but it is important to remember that Jesus was persecuted and executed by religious leaders who failed to recognize any connection between their traditional ceremonies and the spiritual power Christ exhibited.

Regardless of some of my own disappointing experiences with certain groups, I did gain valuable scriptural lessons and guidance along the way. And I must acknowledge in fairness that Christ's teachings were kept alive for many centuries in spite of the sometimes horrible hypocrisy of the church.

One of the great scriptural insights I found quite early was the distinction between *soul* and *spirit*, a difficult concept that, once understood, provides a cascade of *eurekas*. The ancient Hebrew and Aramaic words for *spirit* were *ruwach* and *pneuma*, meaning "breath" or "wind," which God breathed into all living things. The words for *soul* were *nepesh* and *psuchee* (root of "psyche"), which referred to the center of one's emotional self. The picture I get is of God's great wind of creation swirling into diverse, smaller twisters to become *individual souls*. It would account for our egocentric tendency to perceive ourselves as separate beings, each revolving around our own life's concerns as the center of our own universe. It explains our ineffectiveness to see the bigger picture of life from the limited perspective of our own soul, without reconnecting somehow to the original source of God's Spirit. One of life's great philosophical questions arises from this quandary: Why would an all-wise God create individual beings with *free will*, capable of evil choices and apparently born without an automatic connection to the source of infinite love and wisdom? And would He *really* allow us to drift aimlessly forever without providing some way of willfully reconnecting to that original source? The implications of free will are so important that we will return to the question in stories to come.

The scriptural insights into what had happened to me spiritually on that day at the beach led to another way of exploring—through direct life experience. This involved becoming open to personal and interactive experiences through prayer, meditation, and the power that Jesus talked so much about, the *Spirit of Truth, Counselor, Holy Spirit.* These are the tools that I found most useful when trying to understand spiritual things with my heart, to supplement the knowledge of my mind.

While my spiritual life was blooming, my filmmaking interests were taking root. Since both of these great discoveries happened within a span of six months, I sensed early that film would be a special mission in my life. *Somehow,* I thought, *film will allow me to create heavenly visions for earthly eyes.* Within that first year, we produced a film called *How to Break the Habit in Four Easy Shots,* about a burglar who gets shot in the act and sees his life flash before his eyes as he lies dying (this was five years before the first popular books discussed the "life review" of persons who had been revived from near-death experiences). Seven years later, after reading a groundbreaking new book called *Life After Life,* I produced my senior project for the University of Maryland Film School. Entitled *Lit de Mort,* French for "deathbed," it was a special-effect depiction of the near-death experience. This film project not only launched my successful career in animated special effects, but also set the stage for collaborating with Dr. Raymond Moody nearly fifteen years later to produce the definitive documentary of *Life After Life.*

Although I never presented any of these personal background experiences as credentials in the films produced for The Learning Channel, I believe they were vital to preparing me for the task of investigating supernatural phenomena in a manner that was open to discovery of things unseen. It has been a great honor to have the opportunity to meet so many people who have been

touched by the divine, and then to share their stories to a generation of television viewers who are seeking the truth.

I think my sense of being on an epic journey began when I recognized that
small miracles were happening all around us, every day. In fact, as I've said
before, I refer to this journey as an *odyssey* because it is a single story com-
prising many stories. And from every one of those stories reflects a glimpse of
Heaven. But the greatest excitement to me is in realizing that when taken as a
journey, these stories all add up to something, they take us somewhere. So, to
all who read these stories, please follow the clues in this hunt for heavenly
treasure and add the stories from your own life, for they provide valuable
clues as well. This is a quest worth taking.

A Mother's Prayer

mir-a-cle (*mir-'a-kal*) n. ,**1**. *An event that appears unexplainable by the laws of nature and so is held to be supernatural in origin or an act of God.*
— WEBSTER'S ILLUSTRATED ENCYCLOPEDIC DICTIONARY
(BOSTON: HOUGHTON MIFFLIN, 1987)

EGARDLESS OF OUR PERSONAL BELIEFS about religion or the super-natural, we all recognize when certain things happen that break the rules of everyday life. When something out of the ordinary happens—whether you call it a miracle or a coincidence—it can stop you in your tracks and make you take notice.

One story we included in the 1996 TLC program *Stories of Miracles* was an incident that happened to my own mother and sister, and has become a legacy to our family. What follows is Mom's story.

THE PERFECT HOUSE

"It was a sunny afternoon in early spring as I drove slowly around my little neighborhood in Falls Church, Virginia. I loved to drive and I enjoyed look-ing at all the cheerful homes with their daffodils smiling back at me. Today was not just a Sunday-kind-of-drive for me, though. I was on a mission . . . in search of a house for sale. I didn't know it then, but I was also looking for a miracle.

"Since the death of my husband, Houstin Shockey, in 1991, I have lived alone in a very comfortable condominium. My life was full. Activities involving my church, having friends come to visit, giving French lessons, as well as reading and creating artwork made my days most enjoyable. But, by far, my biggest pleasure came from spending time with my daughter, Christine, her husband, Danny, and especially my two grandsons. They lived about twenty-five minutes away and we saw one another quite often. In fact, I baby-sat for the boys several times a week while Christine worked, and I liked being 'on call' whenever she needed me. More than once, though, I had wished that they lived just a *little* closer.

"So I was filled with great hope one evening when I heard Christine casually say that they were thinking of looking for a new house. They were considering a third child at the time and felt that their present home was just too small to handle all the activity. I'm sure my eyes must have twinkled. I made no comment then, but I immediately began having visions of them living in the quiet little neighborhood located just behind my condominium complex. *Oh, what a joy it would be to have them so close!* I relished the thought. Still, I knew it was a rather dreamy notion. Most of the houses in my area were extremely small. But despite these doubts, I could hardly wait to get in my car and go in search of *For Sale* signs.

"I had been driving around for about an hour when a white house with black shutters caught my eye. A rather large home with an inviting yard, it was located on a cul-de-sac, and it was only *five minutes* from my condo. My heart raced a little as I visualized my grandchildren playing on the front lawn. There was something about this house that spoke to me. In fact, this was not the first time I had noticed the home. Several years earlier it had been for sale and I remembered thinking at the time that it would be a great house for Christine's family. It was so perfect. There was just one problem—it wasn't for sale.

"As I sat in my car and looked at that house, I felt an overwhelming urge to pray. *Lord, I know that what I'm asking is a little silly because this house is not for sale. Obviously, people are very happy in that house . . . but do You think that You could put it on the market?* A peaceful feeling gently rested on my spirit after that prayer and I drove on home.

"Two days later I was washing dishes when my daughter called. In an excited voice she told me, 'Mom, we have made an offer on a house.' Astonished, I said, 'Already?'

"As happy as I was for Christine, I felt my own heart sink a little as I saw visions of my dream house vanishing. But trying to sound upbeat, I asked, 'Did you find something really good?' And she said, 'Yes, I think we did . . . and, Mom, it's not very far from you.'

"My curiosity was aroused a little. 'Not far from me? Where is it?' I inquired.

"'Well,' she said, 'it's on a cul-de-sac.'

"*Hmm . . . Could it be?* I thought. Now I was really curious. 'Christine, could it be a white house with black shutters?' I asked hopefully.

"My daughter gasped. 'Yes. How did you know?'

"I said, 'But, Christine, it's not even for sale!'

"'Well, it's *going to be for sale,*' she said, still a bit baffled by my familiarity with the house, '*in two days.* My college roommate lives a few doors down from it and she told me that the neighbor told her it was going to be put on the market in two days.'

"My head was reeling. I knew in my heart that it was the *same* house. It had to be . . . *God had answered my prayer!*

"And it was *true.* Several months later I found myself relaxing in a chair on the lawn of a beautiful white house with black shutters, watching my grand-children play. It was just as I had envisioned that day in the car. My daughter was now expecting her third child and life for me at that moment seemed especially good.

"I always marvel at the way God's hand moves throughout our lives and how little miracles can mean so much. I'm sure someone might say, 'No, that wasn't really a miracle. It was just a coincidence.' But I am convinced that it was an answer to prayer. I was not in a terrible need when I prayed. I wasn't just begging God to meet a need of my children. It was a prayer that came spontaneously to me when I was in front of that house. And that makes me think of the letter of Paul to the Corinthians. He said that we don't always know how to pray and that if we are open to it, the Holy Spirit *prays for us.* I think the Holy Spirit put that prayer in my mouth."

∾

I have told my mother's story to many people who sometimes respond, "I've had an incredible coincidence happen to me also," and then go on to describe one of these *small miracles,* as I have come to think of them. Although the word "coincidence" is frequently met with, "I don't believe in coincidences—I know God is behind everything," there are many people who don't even recognize coincidences at all, and wouldn't if they tripped over one. I believe a sensitivity develops in those who recognize a pattern in life, when dissimilar events are understood to be linked by a prayer or an intention.

When my mom, who was a professional textile designer, was asked how she could possibly account for the chain of events surrounding her story, she said simply, "We are not alone in the world, and I think we are part of a huge tapestry of interrelations."

The following story was told to me by a gentleman from Nebraska. It displays a marvelous tapestry.

BEATRICE, NEBRASKA—MARCH 1, 1950

Herb Kipf glanced at the clock ticking quietly on his desk. *Oh, no,* he thought, *I'm really going to be late for choir practice tonight.* Quickly, he scanned the letter he had been writing to the denominational headquarters located in Chicago. It was an important letter. He *had* to get it finished so he could drop it in the mailbox on the way to church. He licked a stamp, grabbed his coat, and was gone.

Driving to the church, he thought about his fellow choir members and how well the small group of thirteen members harmonized—in more ways than one. He really enjoyed their Wednesday night meetings. He then reminded himself that they were also a very punctual group. He would need to hurry . . .

As he approached the west side of town, he was immediately struck by the fact that the whole area was completely dark. There were no lights anywhere. A funny feeling settled in the pit of his stomach. He wondered, *What in the world could have happened?* Up ahead he could see shadows of people scurrying past the headlights of cars parked at crazy angles near the church. Herb realized something was dreadfully wrong. He parked about a block away, and slowly made his way through the blackness to the church parking lot. His eyes strained against the night trying to make out the strange shape before him. Suddenly, to his horror, Herb realized that he was looking at the church steeple—lying in the spot where his car was usually parked.

Other people, appearing from out of the night, began to gather at the site with flashlights. In quiet voices they spoke about the horrific explosion they had heard only minutes earlier. As battery-powered beams of light darted through the darkness, an awesome sight was revealed. The West Side Church was in ruins.

When the fire department arrived at the scene, Herb was immediately enlisted to provide a head count of survivors so they could determine who was missing. Firefighters searched the rubble while Herb scanned the parking lot for any familiar faces.

One by one, choir members began to appear in front of the site of the disaster. Each of the fortunate late arrivals were dumbstruck by the nightmarish wreckage. What had once been their choir room was now entirely flattened. Those lucky enough to get there late stood in silence watching the firefighters search for victims. They knew in the back of their minds that some friends were beyond hope—the ones who, unfortunately, made a habit of showing up fifteen minutes early for practice each week. Grief overcame them as the sickening suspense worsened, as they waited for victims to be uncovered.

Then Herb's voice rang out from their midst.

"They're all here!" he shouted excitedly. He had accounted for each and every one of the choir members, including the choir director. Incredibly, every one of them had been detained by an unexpected and peculiar setback, just as Herb had been. One woman had spilled something on her dress and had to change. Another family was delayed because someone didn't want to miss the finale of a TV show they were watching. Herb's cousin Harvey and his boys were late because they lost track of time over dinner conversation, and lingered a little too long. There were still others whose stories were similar. Every single member was alive and unhurt, each one having been delayed just long enough to escape the terrible explosion.

When it dawned on everyone what had happened—that a miracle had taken place—the small group gathered in a circle in the parking lot, holding hands, and joyfully gave thanks to the Lord.

It was learned later that the explosion at the West Side Church was caused by a gas leak. Daylight revealed that the blast had blown out the sidewalls and that the roof and flooring system had fallen into the basement. Because of the explosion, the power supply in one section of town was knocked out, leaving clocks frozen at 7:27 . . . exactly three minutes before the choir rehearsal was to have begun.

News of the incident spread far and wide—the story was written up in *Life* magazine—and the church became a great attraction as visitors from out of town came to see the sight of the *great miracle in Beatrice*.

CHAPTER 5

Meaningful Coincidence

T HE FAMOUS SWISS PSYCHOLOGIST Carl Jung coined the term *syn-chronicity* to describe the phenomenon of meaningful coinci-dence. It is said that over dinner with Albert Einstein one evening, Jung got an early version of the Theory of Relativity and subsequently theorized that the universe is connected by a collective unconscious in which synchronous events indicated a "psychically condi-tioned relativity of space and time."[1] In other words, he concluded that con-sciousness may have some control over events in time and space.

Not long ago, my wife, Stowe, mentioned to me that she wanted to find a set of antique twin beds for the guest room. We went to several antique stores but found nothing in our price range, or that even appealed to us. About a week later, we received a phone call from Stowe's cousin, Kay, in Oregon. "I'm calling because I've been storing something in our basement for the last ten years and I've always had it in the back of my mind that I would like you to have it." Kay, who knew nothing of our search, continued, "Be completely honest with me now. Would you be interested in Grandma and Grandpa's set of antique twin beds?"

1. Vaughan, Alan. *Incredible Coincidence* (New York: Ballantine, 1979), p. 188.

On another occasion, Stowe told me that our electric clothes dryer was broken and she wanted to find a used Kenmore, preferably a gas one this time. Stowe called around to some used appliance stores, but was informed that used gas dryers seldom if ever became available. Somewhat deflated, Stowe was beginning to give me the bad news when we were interrupted by the phone. It was a friend I hadn't spoken to for months, and while we caught up, he mentioned offhandedly, "I'm going to borrow a friend's truck so I can get rid of our old dryer since our new place doesn't have gas hookups." I almost choked, and was sure he and Stowe were conspiring to pull my leg. But no, it was *just a coincidence,* and that night we inherited a nearly new gas dryer—and yes, it was a Kenmore.

These things happen to us frequently, and you must be thinking that my wife sends out some kind of powerful signal . . . which *I know* is true! But I realize that many people experience these small miracles; money in time of need; a job at just the right time; a call from someone you were thinking about. These examples of synchronicity follow us, and beg for explanations.

In the next story, Ken Gaub from Yakima, Washington, describes an incredible event that defies any earthly explanation. It contains what some people would call a double synchronicity, in that it really involved two people's needs. Ken wrote about it in his own book, *God Calling,* and he kindly flew to Nashville where we documented his story.

Heaven Calling . . .

Ken's experience happened to him at a time when his traveling music ministry took him a thousand miles from home. He was at a crossroads in his life, not knowing if he was really helping anyone, and he was looking for a sign.

"We were traveling as a musical family going through Ohio with two big motor coaches. Our family, some others, and a music group were going to churches and conventions giving concerts. I was personally going through a real trying time in my life, thinking, *Where am I? What's going on in my own life? I'm telling other people they can have answers. Do I really have the answers myself? Has God really called me or should I maybe quit and get a job?*

"These thoughts were going over and over in my mind, so when everybody else went to eat, I stayed in the bus and sat for a while. I got thirsty and walked down the street to get a Pepsi.

"As I walked back slowly, I heard a phone ring. And I listened and thought, *What is that?*

"The phone booth near the gas station just rang and rang and rang and rang, and I thought, *That's odd. I wonder why it's ringing like that, maybe it's an emergency or something for somebody close by.*

"So I just went into the phone booth, picked up the phone and said, *Hello?*

"The operator said, 'Person-to-person call for *Ken Gaub.*'

"'Ha-ha.' I laughed right out loud, and said, "You're crazy! That's impossible!'

"And then I thought, *I know what it is. It's* Candid Camera *or a setup of some kind.* So I'm looking around and checking my hair and everything.

"And I heard somebody saying, 'I believe that's him, I believe that's him.' And the operator said, 'Well, is Ken Gaub there?'

"I said, 'Yes, *I'm Ken Gaub.*'

"She said, 'Are you sure?' and I said, 'Far as I know, I'm Ken Gaub!'

"And in a moment I'm talking to a lady who was in a hopeless time in her life and had written a suicide note."

The woman, from another state, had only moments earlier made a desperate plea to God. She had asked to be shown a way out of her suicidal plans. She described to Ken that she immediately saw his image in her mind, recalling that she had once seen him on a television show. She remembered how wonderful his ministry was and how his words had spoken directly to her heart that day. She then thought, *If I could just talk to that man from TV—but how would I ever find him?* No sooner had this thought passed than another image appeared. She began to see a string of numbers in her mind. She wrote them down on a piece of paper and thought to herself, *Could God really be answering my prayers by giving me that minister's office number?* Thinking that she might be calling his West Coast office, she decided to place the call person-to-person so that she wouldn't be screened by an efficient secretary. Little did she know that she wasn't calling the West Coast at all but did indeed have Ken Gaub's number. Somehow a miraculous feat of synchronization had occurred.

Ken continues, "And I'm thinking, *How can this be?* What are the odds that somebody would call somebody from another state and it be the right phone number and the right guy walking by. I don't know if the odds are one in a billion or what. And so I talked with her and was telling her that suicide is not the answer."

As the woman listened, Ken spoke to her heart once again. He was able to calm her and help her find a reason for living. Ken would stay in contact with her for several more months, counseling her regularly until he knew that her suicidal thoughts were behind her.

"And that story took kind of a turn," Ken adds, "from me helping this lady, to *God actually helping me!*"

Immediately after the incredible phone call, Ken felt a renewed hope for his life and ministry. With his burden suddenly lightened, he had a new bounce in his step as he walked back to his bus and shouted to his wife, "Hey Barbara! God knows where we are!"

The odds, as Ken observes, are mathematically and scientifically against this kind of "coincidence" happening, especially involving two people whose needs are so great. Is it possible that prayer can link two people's needs to provide a single answer? If there is indeed a way in which a conscious prayer can activate a divine chain of events on Earth, it boggles the mind and leaves one to wonder, how in Heaven's name does it happen?

SEEKING DEFINITION

Jung's synchronicity principle would say that the consciousness of the two people affected the universe in such a way as to bring about this miraculous connection. But what exactly happens in this process? And where does God fit into the *responsive universe* theory?

Since I am in the business of reflecting, I would like to offer some observations that I believe tie together some loose ends in various schools of thinking.

Jung offered the synchronicity theory as an alternative to scientific materialism, which had long ignored the existence of a spiritual realm. Science had centuries before divorced itself from religion, partly because the Church had persecuted scientists for daring to define the world as a machine without accounting for the Creator or *unexplainable* miracles. So, Jung proposed a semi-scientific model of the universe which said essentially the same thing that religion had said all along. His theory stated that conscious prayers or intent can affect the material world, but he said it without using religious terms.

Let me say here that Jung proposed some highly charged ideas that have been met with mixed reactions by some religious authorities. Today's biggest hairsplitting arguments between traditionally religious philosophers and the so-called New Age (or New Thought) proponents of Jung's premise—that one's consciousness *affects* reality—focuses on the definition of who (or what) God is. Is God separate from His creation or does the Creator and creation work as one unified operating system?

There was one memorable incident through which the New Age movement (for which I dispute there to be any single definition), gained a bad reputation among religious fundamentalists. It occurred when New Age celebrity Shirley MacLaine came out with an autobiographical book and TV special, *Out on a Limb,* which portrayed her spiritual experiences, culminating with her moment of enlightenment. She ran to the ocean's edge and, whirling with outstretched arms, proclaimed, "I am God!" This scene introduced a semantic powder keg into the spiritual debate. Some argued for Shirley, that she must have meant she realized herself to be *part of* the Creator—a droplet containing all the elements of the ocean. But to the shock of many viewers, they heard her say on TV that *she was God*—the whole ocean, the great "I Am." And that kind of inference widens the communication gap between traditional and nontraditional thinkers.

I believe we can learn by looking at any issue from several perspectives. Spiritually we grow best when finding our own balanced framework for viewing life.

The basic concepts of synchronicity as Jung presents them are solid enough to Western religion. Christ said whoever had enough faith could move mountains (Matthew 17:20). He told the hemorrhaging woman that by her faith she was healed (Mark 5:34). He told his disciples that by faith they would perform greater miracles than his own (John 14:12). Faith does allow changes in physical reality. And miracles might be better understood when viewed through the lens of synchronicity. Jung said, "Synchronicity suggests that there is an interconnection or unity of [apparently] unrelated events."[2] In other words, even though there may not be an obvious physical explanation of what caused a one-in-a-billion phone call, a miraculous healing, or an answered prayer, they do point to an underlying organization in the universe. One in which a person's spiritual faith can have a dynamic effect on the physical realm.

2. Jung, C. G. *Collected Works,* vol. 14 (Princeton: Princeton University Press, 1970), p. 464.

These ideas bring up all kinds of compelling questions. Why is the expression of prayer sufficient to trigger the response? Is there an optimal condition of our heart, or frame of mind in which to pray? What exactly is the mechanism or organization that God uses to answer prayers?

I think that most people who are inspired by nontraditional ideas are actually not far removed from those who hold to more traditional beliefs. Same search, different paths. Neither are atheists. Most of the followers of spiritual interests would embrace the idea that to love *God* and to love *others* is essentially the same ultimate aim. Throughout religious history, huge canyons of misunderstanding have begun with verbal definitions of spiritually abstract concepts. Those who spend time confronting one another's terms for supernatural experiences can miss great opportunities to share their *light* with each other.

So, whether I call my experience with the antique beds and gas dryer a meaningful coincidence or a miracle is of small concern. The point is that something unseen is working behind the scene, and is somehow activated by one's belief in the system. I know that the same Creator who made sunlight to nourish the flowers and seeds to feed the birds has also designed a working system for meeting all of our needs, and I count on that. Religious art historian Bernard Berenson said, "Miracles happen to those who believe in them." When you begin seeing these unusual things happening regularly, you ask, "Do I believe it when I see it, or do I see it when I believe it?"

CHAPTER 6

The Greatest Story

OMETIMES I FEEL LIKE I have the best job in the world. My film-making has led me into fascinating studies of some of the most profound riddles of life and death, and at the same time has given me a thought-provoking overview of human history.

While writing a script for a documentary called *The Greatest Story Ever Painted,* which tells the Gospel story through art history, I did considerable research into the first century and the events that led up to it. I found it revealing to understand the political and social climate of the world in which Jesus was born. It helped me set the stage for that particular film. But at the same time it provided some tantalizing connections to our investigative documentaries of modern-day reports on miracles, angels, and the afterlife.

For instance, today's resurgence of interest in spiritual phenomena comes after centuries of religious decline that followed the Age of Enlightenment, starting at the Renaissance. Similarly, the first century also saw a dramatic revival of spiritual events following a dry spell of just about the same duration, roughly a half a millennium.

The Old Testament documented a great collection of supernatural stories and prophetic revelations during Israel's faithful times. The Hebrew Bible was filled with spiritual phenomena: angelic messages given to Abraham, Moses, and countless others; miracles like the parting of the Red Sea and Daniel being saved in the lion's den; and prophecies about the coming Messiah and the resurrection of the faithful dead. But those reports dwindled to nearly nothing during the four or five centuries prior to Christ. The reason, as told by the great prophets of Israel, is that the nation had all but lost its faith in the God of Abraham.

But when Jesus arrived on the scene at the start of the First Millennium, popular interest in spiritual matters abounded again. Many Hebrew religious groups eagerly awaited the immediate arrival of the Messiah (translated into Greek as "The Christ"), which the prophet Isaiah, among others, had predicted six centuries earlier. Angels were reported throughout the New Testament, for the first time in hundreds of years. Afterlife, resurrection, and the Kingdom of Heaven once again became hot topics of discussion. And miracles were seen regularly, performed initially by Jesus and then by his followers.

To get a clear picture of the religious and political mood of the first century, and how it mirrors our own times, we need to understand what led up to the long-awaited arrival of the man whose birthday marks the year one.

A Quick Sketch of History

History books reveal that since the beginning of time there have been struggles—between the peaceful and the predatory, the merciful and the malicious. These inborn forces have been characterized as *good* and *evil*, the *spirit* and the *flesh*, or even the powers of *light* and *darkness*. Some said there was a battle raging between the *Kingdom of Heaven* and the *kingdoms of this world*. Throughout the world and throughout time, since humanity's "fall from grace," people have wrestled with the proverbial *serpent* inside. And try as they might to overcome their egocentric nature, the evidence of self-worship would wind itself ever tighter around the foundations of civilization, and around the human heart.

Long before the days of Jesus, the custom of human sacrifice had, in many corners of the civilized world, given way to animal sacrifice. These leftover bloody rituals were performed by priests in temples of the various religions. Sacrifices were often meant to appease the gods, who were believed to control the destinies of primitive minds.

The great Egyptian pyramids had already been completed nearly two thousand years before Jesus was born. Since Egypt's early days, there was only one man who was raised above the priests in their sprawling religious temples. He was the living incarnation of the main god of the land, the pharaoh, the god-king. And over the centuries his role had evolved into one of an aggressive conqueror.

The pre-Mayan Indian civilizations known as Zapotec (Zap-a-TEK), and Teotihuacán (Tae-oh-tee-wa-KON) were already well established by the year one and were expanding politically and militarily. They still practiced human sacrifice and had evolved the ceremonies to a gruesome scale. Eventually, the Mayans would develop a religious tradition much like the Egyptian's worship of a human god-king. These developing Native American cultures were contemporaries of two other, simultaneously developing empires: China in the East and Rome in the West.

China was, in Jesus' day, the greatest, best organized, and most civilized political system in the world. The Great Wall had been started two hundred years earlier to contain the Hun invaders from the north. But the great parallel worlds of Asia and Europe were almost totally unaware of each other, and in a typically human way, each thought itself to be the center of civilization.

Rome was the center of the world into which Jesus was born. In the five or six hundred years that came before Christ's birth, Israel had gradually succumbed to the ways of Greek-style or Hellenistic culture, losing touch with its own God-centered beginnings.

AN AGE OF ENLIGHTENMENT

During the dynamic sixth and seventh centuries B.C., Buddha, Confucius, Lao Tse, Heraclitus, Plato, and the prophet Isaiah taught in their respective corners of a darkened world . . . unaware of one another.

In India, Buddha had shunned his own aristocratic heritage in search of a simpler life, and found his enlightenment while meditating beneath a shade tree. He went on to share his insight that *all* suffering was due to the selfish desires of the individual: physical appetites, worldliness, the ego's desire for immortality. The solution was contained in the disciplined rules of the Eightfold Way, or Noble Path of Life, which prescribed mental uprightness, right conduct, and honest living. And although the highest aim was to achieve a selfless state called Nirvana, there was no worship of a single personal God.

In China, Confucius was born from aristocracy, and like Buddha, he was inspired to seek wisdom as a remedy for the misery and disorder in his land. Like Buddha, Confucius prescribed sound rules of conduct through which he envisioned a nobler world, if only the rulers of the world would comply. He searched all his life for a "prince" who might establish this idealistic new kingdom on Earth, but died a disappointed man. "No intelligent ruler arises to take me as his master," he said, "and my time has come to die."

And at the same time, halfway around the world, as if all these seekers were sparked by some universal impulse, the Greek philosopher Heraclitus and other independent thinkers were also seeking *real answers* to the nature of the world we live in. Plato's *Republic* followed with brilliant ideas that challenged people to rethink the foundations of society. His vision for an enlightened kingdom sounded similar to the ideas of Confucius. Plato, as if to echo some universal dream in the human spirit, also searched for a "prince" to implement his utopian state.

Isaiah, the greatest of Israel's prophets, was simultaneously unveiling the plan of God's judgment and salvation. Israel would face the terrible "day of the Lord" for defying God and straying from righteousness. But, through God's compassion, He would rescue them from both political and spiritual oppression. In this coming messianic age, a king would descend from the line of David. The Lord, according to Isaiah, had called the Messiah "my servant," and through His own suffering would achieve salvation in its fullest sense. The Lord's kingdom on Earth, with its messianic ruler and His followers, was the end goal of Isaiah's prophesies.

And so men and women the world over watched and waited for someone to come and save them from the fear, corruption, selfish ambition, and other evils that seemed to plague human beings since the beginning of time. For six hundred years, the anticipation mounted. But despite the universal longing for a noble and enlightened world, it seems that the governing powers always rested with those who fought most viciously to control the lives of others.

STAGE SET FOR MILLENNIAL CHANGES

If we drew a millennial time line, we would see that the time span between the enlightening sixth century B.C. and the year one roughly corresponds to the span between the *Age of Enlightenment* (starting at the Renaissance) and our present day. Both of these periods can be thought of as times of intellectual incubation, when academic reason flowered. In the West, both of these eras are dominated by what are called Hellenic, or classical schools of Greek thought. Under these similar conditions, both time periods also experienced a decline in religious influence, the earlier time involving Judaism bending to Roman ways, and our own time seeing the church's authority giving way to a sixteenth-century revival of Greek-style scientific reasoning.

If the world could be said to have a hedonistic ego, its center during the first century was in Rome. And if Rome characterized the world's ego, Israel had come to symbolize its spirit of salvation—its reconnection to God.

By the beginning of the first millennium, the Roman republic had grown into the second largest empire the world had ever known and was the hub of the world that Jesus was born into. Its tentacles stretched over two million square miles and siphoned the sweat, blood, and spirit from nearly thirty foreign provinces. Israel was the last of all the Semitic nations to become a satellite state under Rome. The Romans occupied Palestine in 63 B.C., and in their customary fashion, installed puppet leaders in both political and religious positions. In 37 B.C. Mark Antony appointed Herod the Great, whose family was not even Jewish, to be the official *King of the Jews.* Mary and Joseph of Nazareth, both descendants of King David, were born during the reign of King Herod and would one day flee to Egypt because of the insane jealousy the ruler directed toward their newborn baby boy.

The millennial mark of the year one, from which we measure time, begins at the birth of Jesus, give or take five years (the actual birthdate is calculated to be 4–6 B.C. So, at our current millennial turning point, we are roughly in a time parallel to the childhood years of Jesus. We are all familiar with the Christmas story, and the expectations which people of His day held regarding the coming Messiah:

> *Do not be afraid. I bring you good news of great joy for all people. Today in the town of David a Savior is born to you; he is Christ the lord.*
>
> —The Angel Gabriel

ONE MAN'S LIFE

Although there are only a few accounts of Jesus from impartial sources, He obviously made a profound impression on at least one secular scholar of His day. The earliest non-Christian reference to Jesus is in the written records of a Jewish Roman citizen, the first-century historian Flavius Josephus (A.D. 37–93), entitled *Antiquities of the Jews:*

> *At that time lived Jesus, a holy man, if man he may be called, for he performed won-*
> *derful works, and taught men, and joyfully received the truth. And he was followed*
> *by many Jews, and many Greeks. He was the Messiah.* —Flavius Josephus

Most of what we know about the details of Jesus of Nazareth is taken from carefully written reports by several devoted students, *Matthew, Mark, Luke,* and *John* authors of the four Gospels of the New Testament. Tradition holds that *John* and *Matthew* were two of the original Twelve Apostles who followed Jesus throughout His mission. *Mark* was a young student of the Apostle Peter. And *Luke* was a doctor and friend of Paul, the great letter writer to the early churches. In their later years, the Gospel writers saw the need to transcribe for future generations the accounts and teachings that had already been spread by word of mouth through the original disciples.

Oral tradition was in those days a well-established and reliable method of broadcasting information to the world. A person's *word* was his badge of honor, and the accuracy of one's information was taken for granted. Those who undertook the task of passing on the Gospel were no doubt deemed honorable men, but they were also something else: They were bravely committed men who traveled from town to town, from one assembly to another, reciting their stories by firelight. They faced a double threat by doing so, risking penalty of death at the hands of Roman political or Jewish religious authorities. And they were undoubtedly gifted narrators whose testimonies spellbound their listeners.

Luke opens his ledger, written as a letter to a friend, saying:

Many have undertaken to draw up an account of the things that have been fulfilled among us, just as they were handed down to us by those who, from the first, were eyewitnesses and servants of the word. Therefore, since I myself have carefully inves-tigated everything from the beginning, it seemed good also for me to write an orderly account for you, excellent Theophilus, so that you may know the certainty of the things you have been taught. —Luke 1:1–4

The chronicles of Jesus' life cover a broad scope of His mission, teaching, and ministry. One unique aspect of His reputation, and the activity that first caught the attention of the public, was the performance of *miracles*. Here is a small sample of the "signs and wonders" accredited to Jesus.

THE GREAT MIRACLE WORKER

Jesus' first recorded miracle was done reluctantly. His family and friends had been invited to a wedding celebration in Cana, about ten miles north of his own hometown of Nazareth. Wedding feasts might have lasted for up to a week, so the host was socially obligated to provide plenty of food and drink. On this occasion, though, the festive atmosphere outlasted the wine supplies, which trickled from best vintage to table wine and finally to nothing. Jesus' mother, Mary, had noticed the host's embarrassment and had an idea. Knowing her son's capabilities, she turned to Jesus and suggested, as only a mother could, "They have no more wine . . ." A bit self-conscious, Jesus looked about and said, "Dear woman, why come to me?" Then whispered, "My time has not yet come . . ." But, as if she hadn't heard, Mary said to the servants, "Do whatever He tells you to do." I imagine Jesus smiled and, with a sigh, looked around the room at the brightly colored tapestries and other festive decorations. He then pointed to some ceremonial stone jars and said to the servants, "Fill those jars with water." After filling them with over a hundred gallons of drinking water, they turned back to Jesus. He said, "Now dip some out and give it to the host." So they did. When He tasted it, the water had been turned into an exceptionally fine wine. The master of the wedding called to the bridegroom and, raising his goblet, announced, "People always serve the best wine first. Later, after the guests have been drinking a while, they break out cheaper wine. But you have saved the best wine till now!" And so the feasting continued. Nobody knew where the wine had come from except for Mary, the disciples, and the shocked servants. Although Jesus evidently wasn't ready to go public, this celebrated event did have an effect on His new followers. The Gospel of John notes, "This, the first of his miraculous signs, Jesus performed in Cana of Galilee. He had revealed his glory, and his disciples put their faith in him."

Thus began a series of the most impressive demonstrations of control over the natural order of things ever attributed to one man. The floodgates opened to dozens of stories of healing the sick, raising the dead, casting out demons, and commanding the very laws of nature. It is hard to imagine the psychological impact that such displays would have today. But its effect on the population of first-century Judea was evidently captivating, because the news spread quickly.

Luke tells a story that shows Jesus becoming a celebrity, in spite of His efforts to keep a low profile. "When Jesus was in one of the towns, there was a man covered with leprosy, a skin disease. When he saw Jesus, the man bowed before Him and begged Him, 'Lord, you can heal me if you will.' Jesus reached out His hand and touched the man and said, 'I will. Be healed!' Immediately the disease disappeared. Then Jesus said, 'Don't tell anyone about this, but go show yourself to the priest and offer a gift for your healing, as Moses commanded. This will show *them* what I have done.'" But the news about Jesus continued to spread. "Many people came to hear Jesus and be healed of their sicknesses, but Jesus often slipped away to be alone so he could pray." (Luke 5:12–16)

The narratives soon portray Jesus walking a political tightrope. He knew that while these "signs and wonders" were gaining the faith of many, news of the miracles was reaching the ears of those who feared a threat to their authority. The Gospels explain, "One day as Jesus was teaching the people, the Pharisees and teachers of the law were there from every town in Galilee and Judea and from Jerusalem. The Lord was giving Jesus the power to heal people." Just then some men arrived with their paralyzed friend, but couldn't get through the crowds to reach Jesus. So they went up on the roof and lowered the man down on a mat through a hole in the ceiling, right into the crowd in front of Jesus. Seeing their faith, Jesus said, "Friend, your sins are forgiven." Stunned by the way Jesus assumed authority, the religious Keepers of the Law muttered to themselves, "Who is this man who is speaking as if he were God? Only God can forgive sins." But Jesus knew the minds of men and said, "Why are you thinking these things? Which is easier to say, 'Your sins are forgiven,' or to say, 'Stand up and walk'? But I will prove to you that the Son of Man has authority on Earth to forgive sins." So Jesus said to the paralyzed man, "I tell you, stand up, take up your mat, and go home." Without hesitating, the man stood up, bent down to pick up his mat and went home, praising God. This gave the religious leaders much to worry about, since everyone realized they didn't possess that kind of authority themselves.

Matthew's Gospel throws oil on the Pharisees' fire, adding "When the crowd saw this, they were filled with awe; and they praised God, who had given such authority to men." (Matthew 9:8)

The account of Luke shows that even John the Baptist, the prophet who had prepared Israel for the immediate arrival of the Messiah, needed proof for himself. While awaiting his own fate in the prison of King Herod, John sent messengers to Jesus to confirm once and for all that Jesus was really the Christ. The men announced, "John the Baptist sent us to ask of you, 'Are you the one who was to come, or should we expect someone else?'" As a sign of proof for them, before their eyes Jesus cured many who had disabilities, sicknesses, and evil spirits, and gave sight to many blind people. Then he smiled and said to the messengers, "Go back and report to John what you have seen and heard: The blind receive sight, the lame walk, those who have leprosy are cured, the deaf hear, the dead are raised, and the good news is preached to the poor."

Active faith was central in the Gospel accounts of miracles. The faith that Jesus is reputed to have inspired was not just a belief in an idea or concept, but a certainty in the reality of God's power. It was the kind of faith that would make a blind man jump into a crowded street and fumble toward the one whom he knew could heal him, as written about in Mark's account: "Jesus asked, 'What do you want me to do for you?' The blind man said, 'Rabbi, I want to see.' Jesus said, 'Go, your *faith* has healed you.' Immediately he received his sight and followed Jesus along the road." (Mark 10:51–52)

We have no way of knowing how many miracles Jesus might have performed in His lifetime. At least thirty-five miracles, or "signs," as John calls them, are included in the Gospels. John, however, says that *not all* of Jesus' miracles were recorded. "Jesus did many other miraculous signs in the presence of his disciples, which are not recorded in this book," writes John. "But these are written that you may believe that Jesus is the Christ, the Son of God, and that by believing you may have life in his name." (John 20:30–31)

The degree of faith that Jesus demonstrated defies the limits of the logical mind. One story has Jesus saying to His followers, "Let's go across the lake." They boarded several boats, left the crowds behind on the shore, and launched across the great Sea of Galilee. Sometime that night, a gale-force wind came up and huge waves began overtaking the boat in which Jesus was a passenger. He was still sleeping peacefully, "with his head on a cushion" in the stern when His frightened disciples woke Him. "Teacher," they shouted, "don't you care that we are drowning!" Without saying a word to the panicked crew, Jesus stood up on the deck and spoke directly to the wind and the waves. "Quiet!" He commanded, as to an unruly child. "Be still!" Then the wind stopped and it became completely calm. Jesus said to His followers, "Why are you afraid? Do you still have no faith?" The followers were shocked and asked one another, "Who is this? Even the wind and waves obey him!"

Why did Jesus do miracles, anyway? In the records of John, Jesus makes it clear that He did miracles with one thing in mind: "Unless you people see miraculous signs and wonders, you will never believe." (John 4:48) And what He wanted people to believe was His ability to reconnect them to God. "Believe me when I say that I am in the Father and the Father is in me; or at least believe on the evidence of the miracles themselves."

One of Jesus' most compelling predictions foretold future miracles and His designs of linking people directly to God's energy. "I tell you the truth, anyone who has faith in me will do what I have been doing. He will do even greater things than these, because I am going to the Father. And I will do whatever you ask in my name, so that the Son may bring glory to the Father.

You may ask me for anything in my name, and I will do it." This promise was followed up with many biblical reports of miracles performed by the disciples after the death and resurrection of Jesus.

૦૦

All of the miracle stories in the Gospels present readers with the task of believing in something *unbelievable*. To those who walked with Jesus and witnessed His miracles firsthand, it must have seemed just as hard to believe as for those who heard about it one generation later. And for us today, as for the past hundred generations of searchers who have been challenged to believe the unbelievable, many still find it impossible. But others say they have encountered that mysterious force for themselves; the same energy that was reported to have expressed itself through Jesus of Nazareth. Even to this day people are reporting the effects of that miraculous power which reveals itself in undeniable, yet forever mysterious ways.

CHAPTER 7

Feeding the Multitudes Today

∾

NOWHERE HAVE I SEEN God's light shine any brighter than at the Jesuit mission called *the Lord's Ranch* located in Mesquite, New Mexico. I first read about the place in *Guideposts* magazine, in connection to a miracle that had occurred there, and I knew I had to include the account in the TV show, *Stories of Miracles*.

I called the *Guideposts* editors John and Elizabeth Sherrill to ask if they would introduce me to Father Richard Thomas, the priest who heads up the mission. At the time of my call, they were (coincidentally?) back at *the Lord's Ranch* collecting more stories for upcoming issues. It seems that miracles have a tendency of occurring quite regularly there, which I was about to experience firsthand.

Finally reaching Elizabeth Sherrill in New Mexico, she did me the great favor of introducing me to Father Thomas, and an even greater favor by convincing me that *I had* to go there myself to see what was going on in person. Ordinarily, I would have asked Father Thomas to fly to Nashville for an interview, but Elizabeth's enthusiasm quickly convinced me that the trip would be worthwhile. Besides, the good priest might never have time to visit me. He only stops working when everyone's needs have been met. And for the poor people that he attends, the needs are never ending.

Upon landing in El Paso and loading our gear into a truck, I began the forty-five-minute drive into the desert with Matt Coale, the cameraman. From out of nowhere, it seemed, the wind picked up and blew sand over the highway. We watched, in awe, as the sky grew angry and dark, illuminated occasionally by brilliant displays of lighting up ahead. Soon, our vehicle was lashed by ominous, whipping blankets of rain that tried to push us off the road. And as we approached Mesquite, a mere dot on the map, the rains quieted and eventually stopped. Still clenching the steering wheel, I looked in the rearview mirror at the black clouds. Impressed by the dramatic desert sky, I remembered an important shot that I had in the script, which I planned to do as a special effect. "Matt," I began, "let's unpack the camera quickly so we can get a picture of that dark sky. I need the shot to *superimpose a rainbow* when we get back home." A few moments later, we turned into the driveway and passed under the sign for *the Lord's Ranch.* And as we entered the gates we saw directly ahead of us, like a big welcoming sign, the most beautiful *double rainbow* I have ever seen in my life!

The rainbow was just a sign of things to come. "A sign," Father Thomas laughed, greeting us and hearing our story, "made to order!"

It couldn't have been a better symbol for the kind of miracles that people at *the Lord's Ranch* expect, and receive regularly. But the story we came to hear had happened twenty-five years earlier, and literally became a foundation there for many miracles to come.

The next day, Father Thomas told us the story of the amazing *multiplication miracle,* as he calls it. And then he drove us across the border into Juárez, Mexico, to introduce us to another man who had witnessed the event. Frank Alarcón, one of God's most faithful servants, was not only there that special day, but lives on the very spot where it occurred, the scene of their miraculous Christmas banquet.

A MULTIPLICATION MIRACLE

The year was 1972, and Father Thomas recalls, "We'd been studying the Bible where Jesus said, 'When you give a lunch or dinner don't invite your rich friends, your neighbors, or your relatives. Invite those people who can never invite you back, the poor, the crippled, the blind, the lame, and your Father in Heaven will reward you.'"

Father Thomas had fed many people at *the Lord's Ranch* over the years but he felt that he never followed Jesus' words quite so literally. So he decided that on this particular Christmas he would really reach out to people. He extended an invitation to anyone in his church who wanted to help. Many people eagerly accepted.

Preparations began on Christmas Eve. Ladies from the church made burritos and tamales. There was a big ham and little bags of Christmas candy along with cakes and baskets of fruit. Frank Alarcón remembers his contribution: "I brought twenty-five bologna sandwiches. That's two loaves of bread, which makes exactly twenty-five sandwiches." On Christmas Day, people bearing gifts of food and drink came from all around and converged in front of Our Lady's Youth Center. They said a prayer, loaded up their vans and trucks, and they headed toward the border.

Crossing into Juárez, Mexico, they were immediately overwhelmed by the sheer poverty that presented itself. Flimsy structures dotted the landscape, populated by the surprisingly joyful faces of people who lived there. Thirty minutes into their journey, they reached the hills where the garbage dumps are located. Proceeding slowly into the dumps, the group looked for a place to set up folding tables for the Christmas dinner. Father Thomas remembers what struck him most. "To my surprise they were all working in the garbage and they had no idea it was Christmas. They didn't know. To them, everyday was the same. There was no Sunday, Monday, Tuesday, or holidays. Every day was the same, Christmas included. They tried to eke out a living grubbing through the garbage."

Frank Alarcón was especially moved. "I've been in war, I was in the Korean War, and I've seen things, you know, but this was really shocking."

"The condition of the people was terrible," Father Thomas explained. "We found out later that every single man, woman, and child on the dump had tuberculosis."

As Father Thomas and his friends began laying out the Christmas feast, people from the dump dropped what they were doing, drawn to the smell of delicious food. At first, there were only a few dozen people, but within the hour the crowds began to swell. Father Thomas was accustomed to estimating the amount of food needed to feed a large crowd, *but he was not prepared for this*. He said, "I had thought there would be about a hundred and twenty. The turnout that day was more than four hundred people. We said, 'We don't have enough food, but we'll share what we've got.'"

Frank took a lot of pleasure in watching the feast. "They'd broken out this big ham and they put it on the tailgate of my truck," he remembers, "and this lady starts to cut the ham and she's cutting and cutting and giving out pieces and I see everybody walking around with a burrito, a tamale, a sandwich, or a piece of ham in their hand and having a good time, just having a wonderful time."

With the arrival of Father Thomas and his caring friends, the mood at the garbage dump had changed dramatically from a feeling of lack to a celebration of abundance. The spirit was festive. As pleased as Father Thomas was with the turnout, though, he was concerned about how long the food would last.

"After a while this young man came to me with a big slice of ham in his hand," explains Father Thomas, "and he said, 'Have some ham.' I said, 'No, there's not enough.' He said, 'Yeah, there is.' And so I said, 'There can't be.' And he said, 'Well, look.' And I looked around and there were all these people that had big half-inch-thick slices of ham in their hands. Well, that didn't register."

Frank watched people piling their plates high with food and also wondered how long they could continue like this. "And I'm looking around seeing all of these wonderful things happening.

"At the side of my pickup on the ground this lady was giving out these little bags of Christmas candy for the kids. They'd get a bag, run out, and put it in a box or paper sack and then they'd get back in line. Well, I figured for sure we'd run out so I hollered down to Jean and said, 'Jean, we're going to run out of candy, look what they're doing!' Well, she couldn't control it—she just shrugged her shoulders."

"I was taking pictures of people with sacks of food," Father Thomas recalls, "and they would come and fill their sacks up, take them home, empty the sacks, and come back for another sack of food."

Father Thomas stopped keeping count when the crowd surpassed four hundred people who came for the Christmas meal originally planned to feed one hundred and twenty.

"Well, it took several hours for all this to penetrate my mind," says Father Thomas.

Frank adds, "It didn't occur to us until afterward that a miracle had happened. Because we knew what we had taken across and we knew what we had given. We saw with our own eyes all the people that were fed there, and then we saw what was left over."

After everyone had eaten all they wanted, and had taken home so many bags of extras, there was enough food left over to bring the banquet to two different orphanages. "That was truly a wonderful, wonderful thing," Frank beams.

But that wasn't the end of the miracle. Father Thomas explains, "This really got our attention and we said, 'Well, if God multiplied that food, that's a sign that we have to go back and help those people.'"

Frank Alarcón was so touched by what he saw happen that day that he took it as a sign that he should stay in Juárez and help the poor people in that town. "That evening when I went home," he recalls, "and I went in my room and closed the door, on my knees I begged God for a job, with tears in my eyes. I was so in love that day . . ."

He left behind a comfortable retirement in the United States and on the very spot where the multiplication miracle occurred, he used his pension money to organize a day care center, a doctor and dentist office, and other services. He now helps run a co-op which sells food and other supplies for ten percent *below* wholesale, subsidized by contributions from private sources. Frank currently lives in a one-room house with a single light bulb and a mattress on a dirt floor. "A super room," Frank told me with a look of gratitude that made my heart weep. The miracle that happened that day was more than just the feeding of the crowds. It was God's way of opening at least one man's heart and showing him how to lead a life of service for others. "It was just a beautiful, wonderful day. I thank God for that Christmas." Frank radiates. "It changed *my life*."

❧

One can't avoid the similarities between the story of *the Lord's Ranch* and the stories of Jesus feeding the multitudes.

We are told in one of the Gospel accounts that the seed for the miracles of Jesus was the compassion He had for the people. When His disciples commented that the crowd of five thousand who had been listening to Him preach were getting hungry, Jesus said, "*You* give them something to eat."

Then they said to Him, "That would take eight months of a man's wages! Are we to go and spend that much on bread and give it to them to eat?"

Despite their precise accounting for what they could afford to give in human terms, Jesus apparently knew of another resource to which natural laws comply. "Taking the five loaves and two fish and looking into heaven, he gave thanks and broke the loaves." His compassion, combined with the heightened faith of the crowd, allowed such a plentiful feast to occur that there was an abundance of leftovers—more than they started with. And that apparently happened on more than one occasion.

CHAPTER 8

The Faith Factor

∾

THERE REMAINS FOR ME some profound but unanswered questions in life. Such as, why is there pain in the world? Why would a loving God allow misery? Gautama Buddah admitted, "Life is suffering."

A great valley lies between the peak experiences of miracles and divine revelation. The truth is that most people's lives are spent in a lowland of routine sameness, or a worse chasm of despair. Many people, even with an abiding faith in God, go through terrible times of suffering and seemingly unanswered prayers. Why must people endure "the trials of Job," like that Old Testament holy man whose world collapsed around him? Why would a life like Christ's involve a torturous execution? Perhaps it is for our own good that we are allowed to experience the tough consequences of this cause-and-effect world. Or perhaps it is for the good of others. Who can say?

We are often moved by stories of survivors, those people who have endured incredible hardships. Their stories stir something deep within— maybe the realization that it could happen to us. When someone else has lived the very life we strive for, then loses everything; when faith is all that's left, and then even that faith is tested, our beliefs and priorities become naked, exposed.

I read about a Texan in Jodie Berndt's book *Celebration of Miracles*. Upon contacting Jodie, she introduced me to the gentleman by phone, and he agreed to fly up from Houston for an interview. Here is his inspiring story.

AT A LOSS FOR WORDS

In the winter of 1990, Duane Miller, the senior pastor of First Baptist Church in Brenham, Texas, was a man who had almost everything he ever dreamed of. He possessed a deep love for singing and for sharing the Word of the Lord, often building his spirited sermons around a particular message in a song. He had a wonderful family life with his wife, Joylene and their two college-age daughters. For the most part, he even enjoyed the long hours he put in regularly at his church. But on the morning of January fourteenth, he also had other things: a scratchy throat, along with two sermons to preach. This is where his troubles began.

From the moment he woke up, Duane knew that it was going to be a tough day. "It was one of those Sundays," he remembers, "I would've loved to have crawled back into bed and pulled the covers over my head, but I had to preach." So with a stuffy head, an achy body, and a throat so raw and sore he could barely swallow, he wearily headed off to church.

With a cup of hot tea by his side, Duane somehow managed to make it through the first service, though singing was next to impossible. "Every sound and inflection grated on the back of my throat like sandpaper," he recalls. During the eleven-o'clock service he dropped the singing entirely and, bracing himself, concentrated on just getting through his outline as best he could. At around noon, as the congregation filed out of the church, Duane Miller headed home to put himself to bed.

A powerful bout of the flu kept him down for the next ten days. And then, finally, it was over. But the strange soreness in his throat remained. "I was left with a pressure in my throat," he explains. "It was as if someone had my wind-pipe between his thumb and forefinger and was squeezing it." To those around him, it sounded as though he had a bad case of laryngitis. Seeking relief, he went to a specialist. By that time his throat was so swollen with infection that the doctor was unable to get a scope down to examine it.

The doctor's immediate diagnosis was that the flu germ had penetrated the protective myelin sheath around the vocal cords and destroyed them. His prognosis was grim: Duane would probably never have a normal voice again. But the doctor admitted there was also the possibility he might be wrong. Given that bit of hope and some medication to take for the swelling, Duane went home to recuperate.

After fourteen days, the swelling, along with the soreness, disappeared. Duane's voice, however, did not return. Beginning with a team of doctors at Houston's Baylor College of Medicine, Duane began visiting what turned out to be the first in a long line of specialists. Thinking his condition might possibly be stress related, the doctor recommended that the minister take a leave of absence from his church. His advice: take it easy and be totally silent—*for six months.*

Surely, being sentenced to silence would be difficult for anyone, but for a man who loved to sing and preach the Word of God regularly, this was a serious disability. During this time Duane prayed fervently for his own healing, often wondering what God had planned for him. He had faith that he would be healed, but he couldn't help but wonder, *When?*

Six months went by, and there was still no improvement. In fact, other symptoms, such as occasional blurred vision and a loss of equilibrium, developed. Doctors searched for answers. Multiple sclerosis, epilepsy, as well as other illnesses were considered and then ruled out. They were certain of only one thing: The fatty tissues, or "false cords," that were responsible now for his raspy speech would ultimately wear out. Within a year or so, Duane would be completely mute.

With this heartbreaking news, Duane had no choice but to resign his position as senior pastor. With tears in his eyes and a voice no louder than a whisper, Duane Miller said a loving good-bye to his congregation. He and his family then returned to First Baptist Church in Houston, where Duane had served for twelve years prior to going to Brenham. Here, in his most desperate time of need, he was surrounded by old friends who lifted him up in their prayers as well as their hearts.

Duane found himself struggling daily with the realization that he would never preach or sing again. But the question that weighed most heavily now was, *How does a man with no voice support his family?*

The Millers rallied. Joylene and the girls found jobs, and eventually Duane, too, landed a job doing title research for the legal department of a federal agency. His job required little spoken communication and for a while things began looking up. Then suddenly, and for no apparent reason, he was let go.

Months later he would learn the truth from a fellow employee as to why he had been dismissed. He was told that the company's lawyers were concerned that they might have to put Duane on the witness stand at some point and that his voice might be a problem with the jurors.

Day by day, life seemed to be crashing in around him. Without warning, his medical insurance coverage was dropped after the company discovered that doctors had given him no expected time line for recovery. At almost the same time, Duane's disability income was also terminated. He was told that since he was not completely disabled, he could no longer qualify for the benefits.

Summoning his courage, Duane decided to put his hand to writing. A book, he thought, would be a wonderful way to communicate without speaking. He put together a book proposal and, with a small prayer, sent it off to two publishers. Their responses were nearly identical. They both loved his idea, but in order to successfully promote his book he would need to go on a speaking tour. It seemed as if he just couldn't win.

Almost three years had passed and, still, his visits to doctors continued. Baffled by Duane's peculiar illness, specialists from around the world examined the many photos taken of his throat, each one searching for answers. Every little change was recorded and documented, "like time-lapse photography. Every time I would go see them they would put the scope down my throat and record all that," he explains, "so you can watch scar tissue actually form in my throat."

Duane was quickly approaching the time when doctors had predicted he would lose his voice altogether. He was also at a loss for what to do with his life. No matter which way he turned, Duane faced a closed door. Emotionally destroyed, his spiritual faith faltered. He found himself at loose ends and, like many people in a seemingly hopeless situation, began asking God, *Why?*

It was at this time—his darkest hour—that Duane's former Sunday school class approached him about teaching their group. At first, he hesitated, unable to imagine why anyone would want to listen to him speak. But with encouragement from his friends and the aid of a small microphone that he pressed against his lips, he soon decided to give it a try.

On the morning of January 17, 1993, Duane opened the curriculum book. He glanced over his notes on the lesson, which incidentally had been preselected seven years earlier. Then he began the class. The large group of about two hundred people listened patiently as Duane croaked into the microphone, using Psalm 68 to illustrate how God always moves with a purpose. Duane reminded them, "He hasn't changed. That's still true."

Duane addressed the skepticism of scholars who don't believe in modern-day miracles: "On the other hand to say that since we don't have anything recorded after the Book of Acts—that miracles ended at the Book of Acts and they never happened again—is equally wrong because you have put God in a box both ways. He doesn't want to be in the box."

Then, moving on, he asked the class to turn their Bibles to Psalm 103. "Here, in verse two," he read to them. "I'm excited: "Bless the Lord, O my soul. One of His benefits is *'He heals all of my diseases!'*"

Looking out over his audience, Duane smiled. Despite all the struggles he had been through over the last three years, his enthusiasm for God's word could not be contained.

He then read from verse four, "And He redeems my life from the pit." Reflecting a moment, Duane said, "Now, I like that verse just a whole lot. I have had—and you have had in times past—*pit experiences*. We've all had times when our life seemed to be in a *pit*, in a grave and . . ."

Duane's words trailed off. Something had just caught in his throat when he said the word *pit*. People looked up from their Bibles, curious as to what had happened. Tentatively, he went on.

". . . and we didn't have an answer for the pit we found ourselves . . . in . . ." Duane stopped again. He could hardly believe his own ears. With each word he spoke, his voice was becoming stronger. There was no doubt about it. He could feel it. Something miraculous was happening. The pressure that had bound his throat for the last three years was suddenly gone!

"I . . . I don't understand this right now," he said, trembling with emotion. "I'm a bit overwhelmed at the moment . . . I'm not quite sure what to say or do . . ." Bewildered, he continued, "It sounds funny to say, *I'm at a loss for words!*"

An explosion of joy swept across the class. Some people wept, while others began clapping and broke into laughter. As people went forward to hug Duane, they began to realize that they had actually been witnesses to an incredible miracle. And even more amazing was that it was all caught on audio tape! In a church of twenty-four thousand members, this was the only class that taped its Sunday school lessons.

Propelled and energized by the restoration of his voice, Duane decided that the best way to show thanks was to continue with his lesson. Afterward, the congregation broke into song with an emotional rendition of the hymn, "Praise God from Whom All Blessings Flow."

"I don't think anyone who was there that day will ever sing the doxology the same way again," he says. "Its truth struck our hearts for eternity."

It was a memorable day. But as Duane is quick to point out, the miracle did not end there. After his healing, he went back to the doctor for reevaluation. Comparison of the new photos with all of those taken since January 17, 1993, proved that the scar tissue that had formed on his vocal cords was now completely gone. His throat was as smooth and healthy as it was before this all began.

Duane still marvels at what happened. "Scar tissue just doesn't disappear! So, even if you could coincidentally explain how I'm able to speak, what happened to the scar tissue? That's the miracle!"

Concluding our interview with Duane for the film *Stories of Miracles*, I asked him how he accounted for the incredible timing of his miraculous recovery in context of the lesson he was giving at the time.

"I have to tell you," he laughs, and with a velvety tone adds, "I'm still at a loss for words.

"The public way in which this occurred in my life was for the purpose of saying to all those around me, 'I care about you as much as I care about Duane. I'm as concerned about your prayers . . . they mean something.' So I tell folks today, 'When you're praying for somebody, don't stop praying, because you don't know when the moment might be that the change will occur. Don't give up. Don't quit. It's not over.'"

CHAPTER 9

Miraculous Healing Energy

There are only two ways to live. One is as though nothing is a miracle, the other is as if everything is.

—ALBERT EINSTEIN

GAIN AND AGAIN, I have heard of healing miracles in which people used expressions like, "I felt a buzzing sensation," or terms such as *vibration, current, heat, warmth, light*, etc. These descriptions all point to the tangible *energy* that affects people when undergoing supernatural healing.

Back at *the Lord's Ranch* I was introduced to Theresa Juárez, a Mexican woman. Although she didn't speak a word of English, her face radiated a joyful message. When she turned to our translator, Father Thomas, I noticed that the back of her head was nearly bald. I was then told her story. Theresa had been diagnosed two years earlier with a deadly disease.

According to Theresa, "They found a cancerous tumor and the doctor said, 'This tumor is completely developed throughout your whole brain. You won't live for even six more months.'"

Over the next few months Theresa underwent a series of thirty-five radiation treatments. The tests all came back with no signs of remission and left her exhausted, depressed, and without hope. She held her young son and cried desperately at the thought of leaving him motherless before the next change of the season.

She so much wanted to live. She prayed and cried until one day someone suggested she go to the local church where a tribute to a miracle—which had taken place in Fatima, Portugal, years before—was being conducted. As she entered the church, all the thoughts and feelings came rushing in at once. The ruthless cancer . . . No medical hope . . . The God of miracles . . . With all of her heart she decided to submit herself to the power of God rather than the death sentence of the doctors. She threw herself before the Lord: *"Please heal me—or do Your will with me."*

The translator reflects the change in her tone of voice. Filled with wonder, she continues, "When I did that it felt like something was pulling my hair and I felt, on the right side of my face, like something was *buzzing*. There was an intense *heat* that came into me! And I also felt like I wanted to cry, I wanted to scream . . . Eventually, they had to take me out of the church because I cried and cried and I kept on crying. And then I finally rested."

Following this mysterious episode, Theresa was fully convinced that she had been healed. "We went back to the doctor the next day and I said I wanted him to do another test. I felt sure that there was nothing wrong with me anymore, but he said 'No. We're not going to find out anything from a test now because your brain is too inflamed.'" But at Theresa's insistence the doctor sent her to the United States for one more test.

When she and her teenage daughter returned for the results, the doctor was preoccupied and asked the girl, "Do you know how to read English?" She said, "Yes, I do." And he said, "Okay. Here's the envelope." Before she opened it he reminded them not to get their hopes up. "Your mother's cancer is incurable and it's throughout her whole brain."

Theresa smiled. "So my daughter opened up the envelope and when she looked at the test results she turned to the doctor and said, 'Look! This test result says that there's not even a trace of cancer left.' The doctor grabbed the paper and read it for himself. Shocked, he finally said, 'Well, the only explanation I can find . . . it has to be a miracle, because I *know* you had an incurable cancer . . . There was no medical help for that!'"

Theresa said, "Well, maybe for medicine there's no answer, *but for God there is.*"

We live at a time in history when the understanding of "energy" has jumped from purely conceptual to absolutely practical. The electricity that powers our industries, homes, computers, and literally every aspect of modern life was a sheer theory when Ben Franklin was born. Nuclear power and quantum physics have only become real to us in our parents' lifetime. Physicists now know beyond the shadow of a doubt that *matter is energy*, and that material reality and all of its structures can be reduced to vibratory patterns. Even the smallest particles revolve around one another in vastly empty subatomic space. What literally gives shape to physical reality is the affinity that subatomic particles have for one another.

Our philosophic framework for understanding the universe is fusing with scientific thought. Yet with mysterious and compelling implications, physics is providing validation of what the many enlightened religious teachers have said all along, that *God is light.*

The conceptual models, or paradigms, that we use to understand life is changing at a tremendous rate. Rather than sounding strange to us, the idea of

God—the Creator—being *light* makes more sense than ever before. Today when we read that Jesus said, "I am the light of the world," we have to ask if he was using more than a metaphor. There is a Greek word, *zoe*, which means "divine life" or "divine spark." John's Gospel uses it to introduce the concept of the Christ: "In him was life (*zoe*) and that life was the light of men. The light shines in the darkness, but the darkness has not understood it." Like parables, the evolving paradigms of our technical knowledge help to develop a frame of reference for abstract ideas such as spiritual energy, or the spark of life itself.

It is amusing to speculate what parables Jesus might have used for our computer age instead of the ones he used for his agricultural society. Imagine the parables of *The Sower of the Seeds* or *The Mustard Seed* in today's symbols: "A Maker of computers designed a wonderful operating platform. He created a magnificent hardware system with integrated software and supplied his own current to power the machines. He even provided users with free helplines, Internet access, and a stack of manuals. But the users, who were very proud of themselves for owning the computer that the Maker had created, preferred to do things their own way. They ignorantly fell into hardware conflicts and used incompatible programs. Some burned out their motherboards. Ultimately they realized they had downloaded a malicious virus that was destroying their hard drives and with them, everything they had ever accomplished. So, turning back to the manual, they found that they could reinstall the original program, the one that the Maker intended for his system . . ."

Energy, light, circuitry, computers, and communication systems are providing new paradigms for spiritual concepts. And the luminescent language that people use in their stories of healing can provide compelling clues to the nature of the very force that makes us alive and keeps us healthy. In the following stories, you will hear many people who echo familiar religious ideas in terms of contemporary understanding.

A Light at the Bedside

While visiting in my home one afternoon, a Nashville neighbor told me about an experience he had several years earlier. Steve Hooper had been suffering from a severe and painful blood disorder.

One night, Steve awoke to an unexpected visitor. "The room was just filled with light, the brightest, whitest light I've ever seen in my life. And at the foot of the bed was a figure." Steve describes the brilliant being. "It was a man with shoulder-length hair, but I couldn't make out any of the features of the face." Steve also saw bright arches of light that resembled wings. "They were folded against the back and stood about a foot above the top of his head."

And then he describes the sensation. "A warmth filled the room, and a feeling of love also filled the room. It filled my body. I could just feel it all through me, working all through me."

The only message Steve heard was, "I am the angel of mercy." And then the visitor was gone.

The next morning he asked his wife Penny, "Did you see or hear anything strange in the middle of the night?"

She said, "No, why? Did the dog wake you again?"

Steve said, "Don't worry about my iron test coming up next month. I know it's going to be okay. I've just had the reassurance that everything's fine."

And it was. Steve's next blood test came back completely normal, which his surprised doctor had no explanation for.

❧

Another gentleman, Ray Bowman, describes a brilliant visitation he experienced in 1984. It began the day he received news that his young sister had just died.

"I immediately got in my car and started to drive to Chicago, and I was upset with God and was asking him, *Why, Lord? Why my sister? She had everything to live for, twenty years old* . . .

"I was so mad. I was just bitter underneath the skin. When I got to the funeral, I was still demanding, *Lord, why did you take my sister?*"

Then a few weeks later, something happened while Ray was preparing for bed. He still remembers the date of March twenty-fifth. "I was in my room, and all of a sudden this light appeared . . . A big, bright light, something I've never seen before, and have never been able to see again. Out of the light a voice said to me, 'Fear not. Your sister is in a better place.' Then the reassuring voice said, 'Sometimes God has to take the best flower in the garden.'"

Ray explains the immediate and permanent effect the comforting words had on him. "And at that moment, I could feel all of the tension, all of the anger just leave my body. It seemed to be real clear, just a clear bright light, something like a new day."

Stories of these shining callers are so common that one day a refrigerator repairman overheard a conversation I was having at a friend's home and offered his own example:

"When I was eleven years old my dad was in an accident. He had an extensive brain injury. He stayed unconscious for a little over a year in Phoenix, Arizona, in the hospital. He had been lying there and they'd been rolling him in sheets to keep down bedsores. He had lost weight and was just a skeleton, you might say.

"But Dad said later that when he woke up there was a brilliant *angel* at the foot of his bed. And the thing about it is, when he woke up that day he got up out of that bed and walked to the bathroom—by himself!"

∾

Deborah Deckelman was a woman facing her own emotional darkness when she was visited by a radiant stranger.

"My experience happened around eleven years ago when I was going through a series of tragedies in my life. I had two close friends who were killed in a car accident. I had a miscarriage and then lost my grandmother shortly afterward. I was also dealing with some painful joint custody problems."

Deborah had contemplated suicide, and on one dark afternoon decided the fastest way to escape her pain was to take the gun from the bedroom drawer and kill herself. But instead, something compelled her to stop and call her husband. He rushed home and after much anguish, they both decided the best thing for Deborah was to admit her into a depression clinic that day.

Shortly after settling into her hospital room, Deborah was alone. She recalls, "I was lying on the bed and sobbing and crying with my hands over my eyes. Then I heard this beautiful voice say, 'Deborah? Can I come around and talk with you?' I took my hands down and looked up to see an old woman. And I said, 'Yes . . .'

"I was still crying when she came around and sat on the bed. She was a grandmotherly woman, and she said, 'I know what you're thinking and feeling right now.' She said, 'You're feeling like you're in the pit of darkness and there's no hope for you.'"

Deborah continues, "And she was right. That's exactly what I was thinking. She knew me inside and out. Then the old woman said, 'But I'm here to tell you, this is what God wants you to do: *He wants you to take just one day at a time and scratch away at that darkness—just a little bit at a time—and you'll see this crack. And in the crack, everyday you do this, you'll see it open and a little bit more light will come through. And do you know what that is?'* She said, *'That is God's love and promise for you. You must go on.'*

"The woman put one hand on my forehead and one on my heart and began to pray. And as we prayed, it was like someone brought the sun from the sky and into that darkness I had been in. It radiated all over me and all through me and I was being embraced by God. I was being comforted and loved in such a way I had never felt before and I looked up and it was just *pure light*. My mind and my heart were healed. The depression was gone, totally lifted! The woman suddenly got up and went out of the door, passing directly in front of the nurse who was coming in at the time. I asked the nurse who that wonderful, radiant person was that made me feel so loved. And the nurse said, 'Who was *who?*'"

No one but Deborah had seen the woman entering or leaving, and according to the hospital, she was neither an employee nor a volunteer.

"I got up the next morning and got out of bed. Going over to the window, I opened the blinds and right there in front of me through the window was this big, beautiful rainbow—the colors were so brilliant and beautiful! It was my confirmation, that God was telling me again, 'See Deborah, my promises are good!'"

The Healing Light

Jeanie Hunter's miraculous story demonstrates a profound encounter with *the light:*

It was a perfect summer day. Just the kind of day one would expect to find while on vacation in Daytona, Florida. Taking it all in, Jeanie Hunter leaned back in her lounge chair and mused, *Ah, now, this is really living.* For months she and her husband had been working together nonstop to get his new business off the ground. The work was challenging and she enjoyed it, but it sure was nice just to get away and relax a bit. Shielding her eyes from the sun, she watched as their ten-year-old daughter, Laurie, ran back and forth to the water's edge, teasing the waves that crashed around her feet. Jeanie couldn't help but smile. *Yep. Life doesn't get much better than this,* she thought.

Just then, Laurie called out to her. She wanted to take a ride on their float. Always game for adventure, Jeanie waded out into the cool water with her. As Laurie sat on the float, Jeanie pushed her out farther, bobbing over the waves to keep her head above water. She was about chest-high when she looked up to see a giant wave breaking right on top of them. Trying to dodge a head-on collision, Jeanie jumped up as high as she could, turning her face to the right. But she was too late. The wave crashed into the side of her head, completely filling her left ear with water.

Making her way back to shore, Jeanie dried off and began shaking her head vigorously, attempting to drain the water from her ear. But nothing came out. It was uncomfortable and difficult to hear. The rest of Jeanie's vacation was spent in a futile attempt to get the water out of her ear.

As soon as they returned to their Atlanta home, Jeanie made an appointment with a specialist. By this time her ear had become terribly infected. He immediately put her on antibiotics, but after a week there was no improvement. She had a history of ear infections, but this was the first one that didn't respond to medical treatment.

As a precaution, Jeanie's doctor ordered a series of X rays. "He thought I was dealing with a cholesteatoma," she explains, "a tumor that would need to be surgically removed." As it turned out, his diagnosis was correct and surgery was scheduled.

Jeanie's personal outlook about the operation was optimistic. Soon she would be able to hear again. She also thought the surgery might finally put to rest the ear infections that has plagued her for most of her life. All this, plus a little time off from work. Jeanie had a way of looking on the bright side.

Despite her high hopes, the surgery did not go well. Afterward the left side of her face drooped considerably, giving her the appearance of a stroke victim. Physicians questioned whether her facial nerve had been cut during the operation. To make matters worse, the nerve to her taste buds had also been damaged. Everything she ate tasted like wet cardboard and she experienced a constant metallic sensation on her tongue.

Depression set in as she realized just how disastrous the operation had been. Besides her hearing loss, which kept her from being able to understand normal conversations, she was also faced with further complications. She was now tormented by a constant roaring in her left ear. This noise was so obtrusive that it became necessary for Jeanie to have the radio on in order to fall asleep. Because her middle ear had become unstable, she experienced constant dizziness. "I could not even walk through a doorway without hitting one side or the other," she relates. This relentless dizziness was also often accompanied by nausea. In addition, there were many times when, without warning, a piercing pain would sear through the center of her head, leaving her with a migraine headache. In short, Jeanie's life had become a living nightmare.

Unable to do even the simplest tasks, she spent her days in bed, either sleeping or trying to sleep. Food that tasted like cardboard was of no comfort and her appetite waned. Despondently, Jeanie watched as her once shapely figure slowly wasted away. She eventually got down to a gaunt eighty-nine pounds over the next four years. Months went by. Jeanie's family, and the rest of the world, went on without her.

Summoning her faith, she looked to God for healing and help in dealing with this horrible crisis, but none came. Instead, she felt discouraged and alone. Over and over she found herself staring up at the ceiling and asking God, *Why is this happening to me?*

Coming to the painful conclusion that her physician was actually making matters worse, Jeanie sought a second opinion at Emory Clinic. The doctor's diagnosis was bleak. There were no medical miracles available for her condition. In fact, he informed her that she had a progressive illness and the cholesteatoma would more than likely recur. Then, as if trying to extinguish any last bit of flickering hope, he added, "You probably feel better today than you will tomorrow." Heartbroken, Jeanie returned home.

She was still reeling from this bad news when she received yet another bombshell: papers by overnight courier. After twelve years of marriage, her husband was filing for divorce. Devastated, she sat alone in the dark and pondered her future. He had left her with no job or income, a twelve-year-old child and an illness that was incapacitating. Jeanie had hit rock bottom and she knew there was nowhere to look but up. In the silence she cried, *Oh, God. What am I going to do now?*

Perhaps this chain of events motivated her to take action in a way that would not have happened otherwise. She had decisions to make, one of the first being where they were going to live. Up for consideration were her parents' home in Kingsport, Daytona Beach, or a new start in Nashville, Tennessee.

As Jeanie sat at the kitchen table one night considering her options, she distinctly felt that the Lord was speaking to her, somewhere deep within her heart. The message that she heard was, *"Your health will be returned to you in Nashville."* She also heard, *"If you felt good thinking that Steve was going to care for you, you should feel better now knowing I am going to care for you."* Immediately, she opened her Bible, seeking confirmation that this message was from God. Turning to Matthew 6:25, she read the words that would become a reality for her life. "Therefore I tell you, do not worry about your life, what you will eat or drink; or about your body . . ." This was a Scripture Jeanie could hold on to. She felt strengthened. Jeanie knew God cared for her.

In November, after putting their house on the market, she began searching for a job in Nashville. She had lived there a few years earlier and reapplied for her former position as a schoolteacher. She was told she could be reinstated. With job in hand, Jeanie found a small apartment, and in January, she and Laurie moved back to Nashville.

Upon arrival, however, Jeanie began to have a feeling that the Lord had other plans for her besides teaching. She felt as though He wanted her to start her own business, one having to do with typing. By now she was learning how to listen and trust this voice within. So, with her eyes once again toward heaven, she made an emotional plea, *Lord, if You really want me to do this, please help me . . .*

And her prayer was answered. With absolutely no business skills to her credit, Jeanie Hunter began setting up her office. Using a hearing aid to assist her in communications and a couch to lie on when her balance failed her, she was able to start her own medical transcriptionist business—with seven employees!

Running an office took every ounce of energy Jeanie could muster. As her bouts of dizziness increased, she was forced to conduct much of her business from a horizontal position on her couch. But this only confirmed for her that God had led her to the perfect job. Looking back, Jeanie realized, "I could never have taught every day because I could not sit up for more than one to two hours at a time."

Along with nurturing her fledgling business, Jeanie cared for Laurie the best she could, making a valiant effort to keep up with her schoolwork and activities. When Laurie had places to go, Jeanie would drive her there and then collapse in the car, waiting in the parking lot until Laurie was ready to go home. She was a woman with very little strength and driving back and forth was not an option.

Regular doctor visits were still very much a part of Jeanie's life. She received little hope from MRIs and CAT scans. Her doctor eventually gave her the news that her tumor was back and she would need another operation. The surgery did not improve her condition, and she further lost the feeling in her head, arms, and hands. By January 1987, Jeanie doubted seriously whether she would live much longer. Preparing for the worst, she took out a disability and insurance policy to provide for Laurie in the event of her death.

Through it all, she had been trying to strengthen her relationship with the Lord by attending St. Bartholomew's, a local church. On the morning of February 11, 1987, a friend called and invited her to a healing service they were having that night. Jeanie decided to attend. As she was driving to the church, she heard the words very clearly: *This could be the last time you drive to the church sick.* Jeanie says, "I knew that this was not my thought." Her heart raced. As she walked up to the church and opened the door, she again had the thought, *This could be the last time I walk through this door sick.*

Unfamiliar with God's healing power, Jeanie sat quietly in the back of the church. She listened as a woman named Delores Winder spoke excitedly about the Holy Spirit. Watching her pray for others, Jeanie seriously wondered, *Could I really be healed?*

An hour and a half went by and nothing happened. She decided to leave. The lady conducting the service seemed to be so busy with other people. Just as Jeanie was getting up to go, however, some girls she knew persuaded her to join them at the front. It was there that the leader of the group, as well as some other women, gathered around and laid their hands on her. As they began lifting their voices up toward heaven, Jeanie bowed her head and prayed aloud, "Father, I ask You to either heal me right now or let me die because I have no life."

Then suddenly, as though a fog were rolling in, Jeanie became enveloped in a white cloud. Effortlessly, she felt herself *lifting out of her body* and she was able to view the scene down below. The women gently laid her body onto the floor of the church. Jeanie watched in wonder. She remembers, "My legs glowed like fluorescent light tubes." Looking back now, she says, "I believe that was the Holy Spirit moving in and removing the illness from my body."

All at once, from the right, came an explosion of brilliant pinkish white light. It spilled out before her and formed the shape of two triangles. From the middle of the light came the words, *"You are healed."* Jeanie gazed at the light and absorbed these words for what seemed like many minutes, awed by the power of the message. And then she felt the words settle softly into her spirit. She knew she was healed.

It was then that she found herself back in her body, surrounded by her friends. Jeanie noticed immediately that although her hearing aid had fallen out of her ear, she was now able to hear the sweet sound of these women praying. She was trembling, and as she put it, "I felt what can only be described as incredible electric surges pulsing through my body." Jeanie could hear. She was no longer dizzy and the metallic sensation on her tongue was gone. She thought to herself, *A miracle has happened—to me!* Four long years of crippling nerve damage, erased!

Afterward, she picked her fourteen-year-old daughter up and took her out to a restaurant. As they ordered something to eat, Jeanie excitedly tried to explain to Laurie about her incredible healing. "When Laurie's drink, a French vanilla and banana milkshake, arrived," Jeanie recalls, "I asked to have a sip. I'll never forget it. The moment I tasted it, it was like having fifteen Starbursts explode in my mouth all at once. I was so excited I could hardly keep from shouting, 'Bananas! Look! Bananas are back!'"

Completely beside herself, Jeanie remembers, "I jumped up from the table and began running around the restaurant telling people that they should try my drink." Jeanie laughs when she recalls, "For some reason, they weren't really interested in doing that." There was no way she could make them understand that she was just now tasting for the first time in four years. Jeanie could hardly believe it herself!

With a heart full of thankfulness, Jeanie eagerly invited God to take center stage in her life. She wanted to build a stronger relationship with the loving God who had healed her. Her free time was spent in prayer and study of the Bible, trying to learn more about the incredible power she had encountered.

With a successful business and a wonderful daughter to care for, Jeanie's life at that time was full of activity. She also felt quite content as a single woman. But as it turned out, God had other plans for her. "My heart softened to consider marriage later in life," Jeanie says. Soon, she met a handsome man by the name of Billy, and six months later they were married.

Since being healed, Jeanie has devoted her life to helping others learn about the awesome power and love of God. The wondrous way in which He changed her life not only brought her new hope, but also an ability to share her newfound truth. She firmly believes that God uses her to help others. Frequently speaking in churches, Jeanie says, "I remind people that God's incredible love is for them, too. The most important part of this healing was *knowing* that we have a God who loves us. *He is tremendous!*"

∽

Those are only a few stories I have heard firsthand whose glowing descriptions of God's healing power have left an afterimage in my heart. And the more I hear of brilliant imagery in contemporary experiences, the more intrigued I become by light that shines from the stories of ages past. Is God releasing the same energy now as He did then? Consider the following biblical scenes:

"There the angel of the Lord appeared to him in flames of fire from within a bush. Moses saw that though the bush was on fire it did not burn up." —EXODUS 3:2

"I looked, and I saw a figure like that of a man. From what appeared to be his waist down he was like fire, and from there up his appearance was as bright as glowing metal." —EZEKIEL 8:2-3

"After six days Jesus took with him Peter, James and John the brother of James, and led them up a high mountain by themselves. There he was transfigured before them. His face shone like the sun, and his clothes became as white as the light." —MATTHEW 17:1-2

"While they were wondering about [the empty tomb] suddenly two men in clothes that gleamed like lightning stood beside them. In their fright the women bowed down with their faces to the ground, but the men said to them, 'Why do you look for the living among the dead? He is not here; he has risen!'" —LUKE 24:4-6

"When the day of Pentecost came, they were all together in one place. Suddenly a sound like the blowing of a violent wind came from heaven and filled the whole house where they were sitting. They saw what seemed to be tongues of fire that separated and came to rest on each of them. All of them were filled with the Holy Spirit and began to speak in other tongues as the Spirit enabled them." —ACTS 2:1-4

"God is light; In him is no darkness at all." —1 JOHN 1:5

So, what do the seemingly unrelated subjects of Scriptures, science, and these contemporary stories have in common? What is the link, if any, between the mystical *light* of religion, and what physicists say about the material world being composed of vibrations of energy or wavelengths of light? How do we square the stories of people who report surges of brilliant energy during supernatural healing and biblical stories that portray God, Christ, angels, and the Holy Spirit with brightly radiant imagery? What implications might all these things have in the relationship between our spiritual and material realities?

To borrow a metaphor from Plato's "Allegory of the Cave," our everyday world may be just a flicker of shadows on the walls of our cave, cast from the brilliant light shining behind us at the entrance door. As Plato wrote in *The Republic*: "*When he approaches the light his eyes will be dazzled, and he will not be able to see anything at all of what are now called realities.*"

PART TWO

Angels

CHAPTER 10

By Angelic Arrangement

NOTHER TV SPECIAL I had the pleasure of producing for TLC was a two-part investigation entitled *Angel Stories*. The assignment was to seek out real-life accounts from people who claim to have been touched by angels. We then sought to contrast those reports with historical information from various religions. And along the way, if there was any objective evidence from science, so much the better.

As to scientific proof, it is hard to come by, because most of the evidence regarding spiritual phenomena is anecdotal. The previous chapter suggested some of the theories of quantum physics as they might relate to the supernatural. I purposely discussed those ideas before this chapter on angels, because of an assumption I will pose here. I theorize that if there is such thing as an *angelic realm*, then it would have to operate at a higher frequency, so to speak, than the *physical realm*. If the basic composition of the universe is harnessed energy, then it also stands to reason that an intelligent Creator would communicate His ideas, and receive feedback, through the fastest possible medium: *light*.

The Greek word, "angelos," literally means *messenger*. At the risk of sounding pretentiously metaphysical, I like to describe angels as *messengers of light*,"[3] due in part to the premise offered above, and partly because they are often reported as radiant beings. Since nearly all of the accounts we investigated for *Angel Stories* were positive in nature—bringing comfort, healing, and compassionate help—I think of the angels in these stories as *Messengers of God*.

From its beginning, *Angel Stories* was followed by unexplainable events. I had presented the idea of an angel program to The Learning Channel. They responded several months later, expressing an interest and asking for a detailed outline. I had ten days to shape up the proposal before the scheduled meeting. The problem was that all the secretaries at Cascom, the production company I worked with, were busy with other projects. Unfortunately, I did not own a personal computer at that time and besides, I still typed by the hunt-and-peck method.

Worse yet, I had no ideas for how to open the film. A good documentary film, I believe, needs to establish its "voice" from the opening, setting the narrator's tone with a human point of view. I like to begin with a story from a sympathetic, but levelheaded journalist or spokesperson. One author of a bestselling angel book whom I had met (and prayed with in her kitchen) was my original choice of narrators. But when the time came, she had already made a commitment to another angel documentary, and I was out of luck. Or so it seemed.

I know I prayed for some way out of my dilemma, but I don't remember exactly what I asked for . . . perhaps an extension to the deadline, a divine

---

3. An interesting footnote is that the Latin name for Lucifer, the legendary archangel cast from Heaven for leading a revolt of the angels, means the *bearer of light*. This leads to some interesting debates about the unreliability of light as a security badge for goodness, not to mention the issue of free will extending to the angelic realm, and the implication of corrupt messages. But we will save this idea of light and darkness for later, viewed through the prism of several stories.

inspiration or *something!* You simply don't let a request from a television network go unanswered when they show an interest in your idea.

I only had to sweat for about a day before I got an amazing phone call, out of the blue. A woman with a pleasant voice introduced herself as Pam Kidd. She had just seen a program I produced about near-death experiences and had the urge to speak with me. Realizing that I lived in her hometown of Nashville, she looked for my name in the phone book and called my number. She told me that she had enjoyed the film, "Especially the part about people's encounters with angels, which is a subject I am absolutely fascinated with!"

Pam explained that she was a freelance magazine writer, assigned by *Guideposts* to submit some stories she had collected about *angels*. One of them was her own personal encounter! She went on to say, "And if you ever need any writing done, I would love to help." I almost dropped the phone.

Here was a creative writer with amazing credentials (*Guideposts* is a prominent publisher of angel stories), with a personal angel experience, a deep desire to help, living five miles from me, and with a computer! Just as important, she had time available in the coming week to do the work. Needless to say, I took her up on the offer. And when TLC contracted for the show, it was Pam's own personal angel story that opened the film. She wrote a wonderful script, and her narrative perspective unfolded the whole collection of angel stories. She was literally God-sent.

That synchronistic experience was one of those *"little coincidences that one files away,"* as Pam puts it, hoping to one day get a clear picture of the underlying cause and effect. I was once given an interesting explanation of what might be going on in circumstances like that one, and find it useful while considering the function or job description of angels.

The following scenario is from a man I met named George Ritchie, a psychiatrist who underwent a near-death experience and claims to have witnessed the behind-the-scenes workings of a vast angelic system. He found himself in the presence of a brilliant white light he identifies as Christ, who escorted him on a tour of various realms of existence (George visited us in Nashville to tell about many things he saw, which we will hear about later in the chapters on afterlife experiences). But his particular glimpse of the angelic realm was one of the most insightful bits of information I have collected.

George first describes two environments he was brought to see before arriving in the angelic realm. It is interesting to note the degrees of light he uses to distinguish humans, deceased souls, angels, and ultimately, the Christ-light in the following realms.

First, he was shown an earthly environment in which living people were individually enveloped by a sort of electrical field, which George called an *aura*. He understood this light to be the life force radiating from their physical bodies. In the same environment, "running counterbias to the physical world," he saw gray, colorless souls with no light or aura, who were deceased persons that couldn't (or wouldn't) leave the earthly plane. Some were bonded to living people through love. Others were earthbound by addictions, compulsions, and worldly attachments. These gray souls were seen to gravitate to living beings with similar addictions or affinities. For example, George saw real [living] people getting drunk at a bar. As the drinkers' aura was weakened by the alcohol, holes would actually open up in their electrical field. When that happened George could see other souls, who had been milling about the bar, rushing into the defenseless body "trying to vicariously experience the sensation of being drunk."

Next, he was taken to an area consisting mostly of those colorless souls who seemed to not only be lost, but consumed by their own selfishness. He described them as being extremely dense and possessed by "the most hateful, vengeful, self-centered, know-it-all attitudes" he had ever seen. "They were bludgeoning one another and committing all kinds of lewd acts on one another." He saw angels there, too, trying to offer help and occasionally getting through to these self-absorbed souls. "And," George added, "the condition of these lost souls seemed to nearly break the heart of the Christ, who was there beside me."

Finally, and in sharp contrast to the previous realm, he was shown the angelic realm. George starts, "They don't have wings." However, the beings there emitted a tremendous amount of light. "Their glow was much brighter than the auras emitted from humans, though not as brilliant as that coming from Christ Himself.

"These beings seem to be in special service to God, voluntarily. But when they come into that service, it seems to be forever.

"I call this the *mental realm*, for lack of a better term. The beings here came together to study music, arts, science—research of all kinds—and to study the holy books of the universe. I saw these angelic beings dressed, oddly enough, in brown monklike garb in a library bigger than all the buildings of a large city combined.

"I have never been anywhere that I've heard such amazing music. I think that Beethoven, Bach, Brahms, and Tchaikovsky would all have been right at home there. There were musical instruments there we don't even have here on Earth—yet.

"I was conducted through centers of higher learning, where I couldn't even understand the scientific instrumentation I saw these beings working with. In fact, ten years after my near-death experience, which happened during WWII, I saw a picture in *Life* magazine of the first atomic power plant and it made the hair on my back stand straight up! Here was an instrument in the picture that I had seen these beings working on ten years earlier . . ."

Dr. Ritchie then described something I found most interesting. He observed that these beings "transcended the realms," in order to bring information to human beings. These angelic messengers were imparting subconscious suggestions, literally speaking, to a receptive person in a dream or other heightened state of awareness. "I know that we psychiatrists cannot explain how new ideas come into the human brain. But I think I know! I think it is in this realm that there are beings already doing a great deal of research."

❧

Could George's glimpse of the heavenly realm offer an explanation of how two (or more) people get the same idea simultaneously? I know that as a creative professional I frequently get an "original" idea, only to discover later that someone else has gotten the same idea at the same time. For example, even though I thought that my *Angel Stories* proposal was a completely unique concept when I submitted it, two other networks released angel documentaries before ours was aired. Stories abound of multiple inventors coming up with the same device at once, practically bumping into each other at the patent office. A good friend of mine named Wayne invented a revolutionary piece of film equipment. I know exactly when he got the "eureka," because I worked for him at the time. Eighteen months later at a trade show Wayne discovered that two other people came up with exactly the same device within weeks of his brainstorm; one in South Africa and one in Hollywood. My friend got along so well with the South African "competition" that they teamed up and enjoyed a successful partnership.

Dr. Ritchie's NDE (near-death experience) literally began an avalanche of studies into the afterlife, angels, and related phenomena. You see, Dr. Ritchie was a professor of psychology at the University of Virginia in the 1960s and shared his story in class. One of his students, a young man named Raymond

Moody, Jr., was so inspired by the description that upon hearing it—and then encountering similar stories elsewhere—decided to write a research paper. The paper led to Moody's bestselling book, *Life After life,* which in turn opened the door to an entire new field of research—near-death studies. The topic has spawned literally hundreds of books with thousands of accounts of NDEs— now a household term—and triggered a popular secular fascination in spiritual phenomena, with a particular emphasis on *angels.*

Catching an occasional glimpse into this divine-message system offers some intriguing insights and brings up other interesting questions about the angelic order. Could their method for delivering information explain other coincidences as well, like my need for a writer being fulfilled by Pam Kidd's inspiration to call me? And what purpose does prayer serve in activating this communication system? Just how much power is bestowed upon these messengers for tasks like healing, rescuing, or appearing in human form? What can we learn about angels from the Bible and from other religious traditions? And how does the traditional concept of angels correlate to the growing number of real-life angel stories?

CHAPTER 1 1

Angel Stories

 HAVE NEVER PERSONALLY SEEN an angel or heard "a voice from Heaven." But my wife says she heard a voice once . . . We know the date, because it was her late mother's birthday. On June 30, 1994, Stowe phoned me at work to tell me about what had happened.

Stowe had been in a conversation with some out-of-town guests when she suddenly heard a voice saying, "I want to have a baby!" It was an audible voice that came from off to one side, but from an invisible source. She was a bit stunned, and bewildered by the first-person use of the word "I," because she had always maintained that she did *not* want children. Stowe silently responded, "No, *I* don't . . ." Once again the persistent voice said, "I want to have a baby." She says she completely lost track of conversation with the houseguests, who obviously hadn't heard anything. Besides the shock of hearing a *voice*, the very idea of a baby met with resistance. Stowe was in the middle of a successful songwriting career and had always voted against having children whenever I brought it up. But for the rest of the morning her memory of the strange voice kept replaying, "I want to have a baby," until Stowe began seriously wondering if *her own heart* was changing on the issue.

All day long she ran into friends and coworkers who were new parents, all gushing about their babies. In the afternoon Stowe called me at the studio and said, "Honey, I think my *bioclock* just went off!" After hearing the story, I thought, *Bioclocks don't have voices, do they?* A little more than a year after hearing that *divine suggestion*, our precious Christina Leigh Shockey was born. And two years later we were blessed with another darling little girl, baby Grace. Looking at my beautiful daughters now, all I can do is smile and be thankful to whoever it was that planted that inspiration.

∿

State Senator Mary Ellen Brown of New Hampshire told me of an odd incident that happened when her son was an infant.

"I was walking him in his baby carriage," she said, "and came to a corner on a busy street . . .

"I was letting the carriage down onto the road because there was a curb, and I heard a voice—a very commanding voice—saying to me, *'Put the carriage back on the sidewalk!'* I did. I didn't hesitate, it startled me so.

"When I got him back up on the sidewalk, I stepped back a little bit—and immediately a truck turned down the street that I was crossing. I hadn't seen the truck. He was going too fast, and he cut the corner so sharply that his wheels came up right over the curb and just missed me and the baby carriage.

"I was so startled as I watched this thing happening . . . It was sort of . . . surreal.

"I looked around to see who had said that warning to me—to put the carriage back—*and there was nobody there!* Needless to say, I was a bit shaken up. I didn't think at that time that it was an angel, but I felt it was certainly something unusual."

MILLENNIAL ANGELS

Exactly two thousand years ago, an angel's warning had saved the life of another baby boy.

"And having been warned in a dream not to go back to Herod, they returned to their country by another route.

"When they had gone, an angel of the Lord appeared to Joseph in a dream. 'Get up,' he said, 'take the child and his mother and escape to Egypt. Stay there until I tell you, for Herod is going to search for the child to kill him.'" (Matthew 2:12–13)

And *exactly two thousand years before the baby Jesus,* yet another angelic message purportedly saved the life of a son who would become the forefather of an entire nation.

2000 B.C. (approx.)—Genesis 22:11–18. "But the angel of the Lord called out to him from heaven, 'Abraham! Abraham!'

"Here I am," he replied.

"Do not lay a hand on the boy," the angel said. "Do not do anything to him. Now I know that you fear God, because you have not withheld from me your son, your only son."

This angelic message precisely four millennia ago marked the beginning of the entire Judeo-Christian heritage, announcing, "through your offspring all nations on earth will be blessed, because you have obeyed me."

The Bible is filled with angel stories with messages of vital information, brought to those who were receptive:

1500 B.C. (approx.)—An angel came to deliver a great message of hope to Moses, in Exodus 3:2. "There *the angel of the Lord* appeared to him in flames of fire from within a bush. Moses saw that although the bush was on fire it did not burn up."

1000 B.C. (approx.)—An angel helped to establish the location of Solomon's temple as a sign of King David's repentance (2 Samuel 24:15–25). "When David saw the angel who was striking down the people, he said to the Lord, 'I am the one who has sinned and done wrong. These are but sheep. What have they done? Let your hand fall upon me and my family.'" It was there, "on the threshing floor of Araunah the Jebusite," that the angel of the Lord stopped the terrible plague which was about to destroy Jerusalem. A message was delivered to build an altar on the floor of that granary, a tribute marking another turning point for Israel. This angelically inspired monument happened just one thousand years after Abraham and one thousand years before Jesus.[4]

4 B.C. (approx.)—Marking the beginning of the New Covenant with Israel, the angel Gabriel announced to Mary that she would bear a son. "How will this be," Mary asked the angel, "since I am a virgin?"

The angel answered, "The Holy Spirit will come upon you, and the power of the Most High will overshadow you. So the holy one to be born will be called the Son of God . . ." (Luke 1:34–35)

And later that year, "There were shepherds living out in the fields nearby, keeping watch over their flocks at night. An angel of the Lord appeared to them, and the glory of the Lord shone around them, and they were terrified.

4. As a note of millennial trivia, Matthew's gospel specifically cites these two ancestors of Jesus who happened to mark thousand-year increments. The first sentence in Matthew's account begins, "A record of the genealogy of *Jesus Christ* the son of *David,* the son of *Abraham* . . ."

But the angel said to them, 'Do not be afraid. I bring you good news of great joy that will be for all people. Today in the town of David a Savior has been born to you; he is Christ the Lord.'" (Luke 2:8–11)

And in our time, too, there are stories of angels who convey messages of warning, hope, instruction and vital information. Often, they deliver an *indirect* message to all who hear the story as well: *"Do not be afraid—God is with us—We are not alone!"*

Listen for yourself to the underlying messages conveyed through the following accounts from real people we interviewed for the documentaries *Angel Stories* and *Stories of Miracles*.

MOUNTAINTOP EXPERIENCE

Sometimes being high atop a mountain can make you feel closer to God. A young college student named Jocelyn Veile went on a mission retreat to the mountain ranges of Uruguay. On top of one of those mountains, in a strange landscape so far from home, Jocelyn had a memorable and life-changing experience.

Jocelyn leaned back carefully on a boulder. Squinting into the afternoon sun, she surveyed the rough and rocky terrain below. What a day it had been. For the last few hours she and a friend, along with a group of other students, had actually been *climbing a mountain* in Uruguay. *Oh, the stories I'll have to tell,* she mused. It was all pretty high adventure for such a young lady. But as she and her partner caught their breath, they decided it was probably time to begin the journey back down.

Suddenly, to their horror, she and her friend looked out just in time to see that the bus that had brought them there, along with the rest of their group, was pulling away. Jocelyn recalls, "We didn't know if they had left anybody there to find us, we didn't know if they even knew that we were there." Panic set in and tears filled the young girls' eyes. "We were both really scared," she says. It was in this moment of distress that both girls reached deep down inside for a strength more powerful than fear—their faith in God. "To try to keep ourselves from going too crazy, we started praying," Jocelyn says. "And we started singing praise songs."

Trusting that God would take care of them, they found the courage to begin their long descent down the mountain. At first, they attempted to climb down, much in the same way as they had climbed up, but this proved to be treacherous and difficult. They finally resorted to sitting on the rocks and scooting themselves forward somewhat like a child on a slide. It was slow going, but they felt as if this would eventually get them to the bottom.

After sliding down in this rather awkward manner for about half an hour, a native man appeared before them, far off the beaten path. "He was a young man," Jocelyn explains, "and my friend and I thought, *Oh, good! Finally, somebody who can show us the way down.*"

Excitedly, the girls began waving and calling out to the man. One of the few Spanish words they knew was *Ayuda*, which means *help*. Jocelyn remembers, "Over and over we were yelling, '*Ayuda! Ayuda!*' and pointing down and crying and screaming." Without a word, the man calmly took both the girls' hands and began leading them to the left. Jocelyn and her friend immediately froze in their tracks. "No, *that* way!" the girls cried, again gesturing down the mountain. "*Ayuda, ayuda,*" they said, trying desperately to make their rescuer understand their wishes. He nodded confidently and once again took their hands and began leading them to the left.

Reluctantly, the girls followed. At least the path that he was showing them was a bit easier than scooting down the mountain the way they had been.

After a short time and much to the girls' relief, the trio began descending the mountain. Jocelyn recalls thinking, "Well, finally he's figured out what we want here, and he's showing us the way to the bottom."

When at last they made it safely to the parking lot, the girls were glad to find they had not been forgotten. "The group had left a translator and my mother there for us," Jocelyn says.

It was at this time that their native guide motioned to the girls. Looking up at the mountain, he pointed to the spot where he had found them. Jocelyn and her friend were horrified when they realized they had been only a few feet away from going over a cliff! "When we saw that, we both just kind of lost it," Jocelyn says.

Appreciation for this stranger's kindness filled the girls' hearts. He had literally saved their lives. They realized at that moment that he had been Heaven-sent. How else could they explain the fact that this man had appeared from out of nowhere to lead them down the mountain?

As they walked to the car, Jocelyn pondered this question. Suddenly she realized the man was no longer with them. She recalls, "We took a few steps, turned around, and he was gone." They quickly scanned the area, but their rescuer had completely disappeared. Searching for any trace of their guide, they looked for clues in the soft sand. "There were no footprints," Jocelyn explains. "We could see our footprints in the sand, but his had simply ended!"

Helping Hands

He will command his angels concerning you,
to guard you carefully;
they will lift you up in their hands,
so that you will not strike your foot against a stone.

—LUKE 4:10–11

HERE ARE SOME MOMENTS IN LIFE, no matter how old we get, which shine brightly in our memory like stars in the heavens. As a young child, Candace Emerson had just such an experience.

CAUGHT IN MIDAIR

In the spring of 1961, eight-year-old Candace was playing on the carport of her family's Tennessee home when she stopped momentarily to admire the enormous woodpile that stood before her. Through the winter her parents had cut down a number of trees on their property, carefully stacking the wood at one end of the carport. Standing seven or eight feet off the ground, it looked like a mountain to young Candace. And she knew what mountains were for . . . climbing! In an instant she was scaling the logs. Nearing the top, however, her foot slipped and she lost her balance. In what seemed like slow motion, she felt herself falling over backward, plunging headfirst toward the concrete floor below. It was at this moment that she recalls, "Strong hands came up and literally pushed me back up on top of that woodpile and kept me from falling." With a smile of relief, Candace turned around, fully expecting to see her mother or father. "I thought they had been behind me and had seen me begin to fall and then run to my rescue to keep me from hurting myself. But when I turned around, there was no one there!"

LOST AT SEA

Don Spann, a good-humored and successful South Carolina businessman, loves the good life. He works hard and plays hard. As the owner of his own company, Span-America, he devoted much of his life to creating products that offer help to people in need, like special hospital beds for convalescence, and unique fire extinguishing systems for gasoline fires. But when it was time to unwind, Don often heeded the call of the ocean and headed South for a little R&R on his forty-six-foot boat, *Perseverance,* a name that, by the way, could describe Don in a nutshell. In the spring of 1993, however, Don Spann would need something stronger than his own perseverance to help him out of the trouble he was about to find himself in.

Don took in a deep breath of ocean air and looked out across the April sky. Beautiful! Having just completed his routine safety check aboard the yacht, Don smiled at his buddy, John Thomson, who traded a thumbs-up. They were ready to shove off. With John-T beside him, Don took the helm, and the boat slowly chugged out of the Charleston, South Carolina, harbor. They were on a two-day cruise to Fort Lauderdale, Florida.

Their first day out was routine, but by noon of the second day the skies had darkened ominously and the waters became choppy. John-T manned the helm while Don sat back in the stern. Oddly enough, although Don was a safety-conscious man, his life preserver lay unused beside him.

Checking the depth finder, Don took note that they were in about eighty feet of water. He then scanned the map. They still had twenty miles to go before they would make land. With the waves rising higher by the minute, the boat rose and fell like a roller coaster. Don tried to stand up. Just then a particularly strong wave smacked against the side of the vessel. In that instant, something told him, *You're going over the side of the boat today, fella . . .* Knocked off balance, he somersaulted over the side, struck the swim plat-form, and splashed into the ocean.

Immediately surfacing, Don waved his arms, whistling and shouting for John-T. "I'm here! Turn around!" he yelled. But Don's calls went unheard, his voice drowned out by the steady chug of the boat's engine. John-T, facing for-ward, was unaware that anything had even happened. Helplessly, Don watched as the *Perseverance* pushed on without him. In just a few short moments, the boat disappeared from sight. Left alone, Don Spann was lost at sea.

Trained in water safety, Don knew the first thing he had to do was remain calm. *Conserve your energy*, he told himself. Certainly John-T would notice his absence and come looking for him soon. All he had to do was wait patiently. But fifteen minutes passed, and there was no sign of the boat.

Bobbing along helplessly in the waves, he tried to calmly assess his situa-tion. "I didn't have anything to help me," he explains. "I didn't even have on a pair of long pants to cross and tie the legs to use for flotation as they teach in lifesaving." Don would have to keep himself afloat by treading water. But flailing around in the ocean is risky business. "I was in with fish that were big enough to consider me part of the food chain, and I didn't have a weapon," he relates. Besides his fear of attracting sharks or marlins, Don also faced another, more impending enemy. Hypothermia. The springtime waters were cold. In order to stay warm, he would have to keep moving—sharks or no sharks.

Don scanned the horizon. *Come on, John-T . . . Where are you?*

Forty minutes went by. His arms and legs were heavy now and his breathing labored. As Don floated along in the water, his mind, too, began drifting. He thought lovingly of his family. How would his wife and children take this news that he was lost at sea?

A dark loneliness descended upon him. He realized how small he was in the scheme of life. Just a tiny speck, adrift in a deep sea beneath an even larger sky. He had nowhere to go but within, to the depths of his soul. And so, for the first time in years, Don Spann thought about God. He relates, "It's such a temptation to say, 'God, if You'll just get me out of this jam I'm in right now, I'll be a good boy the rest of my life.'" But Don could not do that. He felt it was not right to start bargaining with God in this, perhaps his final, hour.

Still, he did feel compelled to ask at least one last favor. Don humbly prayed, *God, if it's Thy will, and if I'm allowed, may I have Your permission, Lord, that I get at least just one foot on a sandy beach, and then if I fall over dead, that's fine. But please, don't take me this way . . . if I may ask.*

Suddenly, Don heard a deep voice. Could it be God? No, this voice sent a chill right down to his very soul. "Don," it coaxed, "you're not going to get out of this situation. Why don't you relax and die peacefully?"

Frightened, Don ignored the voice at first. But it came once more, this time commanding him, "Give up, it won't hurt."

Don answered out loud. "No! I'm going to fight!"

Don had made the voice angry. It echoed loudly in his ears, taunting him. "Don," it hissed, "give up. John-T is *not* coming back."

Don knew immediately that the voice was wrong. And he shuddered to think who it was that was trying to deceive him. Incensed by the thought of giving up, Don shouted to the voice, "I won't give up . . . even if I'm ten feet under." And for good measure, he added, "You got that, fella?"

Don's voice echoed across the waters. And then silence. He was alone again. He suddenly found himself feeling a bit embarrassed. "I realized I was talking to a *voice* . . . and I'm by myself out there!" He couldn't help but wonder, *Have I lost my mind out here in the middle of the ocean?*

Nearly an hour had passed. Don was exhausted and losing his battle to stay afloat, at times sinking beneath the waves. He couldn't hold on much longer. And then, in his state of semiconsciousness, he heard something that roused him. To Don Spann, it was the most beautiful sound in the world—a deep rumble . . . *blum, blum, blum.* He recognized immediately the sound of his boat. "That was old *Perseverance!*"

Even from a distance, between the swells and crests of the waves, Don could see the figure of John-T scanning the horizon with binoculars. Don watched intently. Suddenly, John-T lowered the glasses, then quickly raised them up again. *Oh thank God! He sees me,* Don thought. John-T shouted across the water to him. "DON!" he called elatedly. Relieved at finally being located, Don says, "I think, just for a moment, I partially blacked out."

But John-T's shouts brought him around again. "Catch the line!"

Wearily, Don reached for the rope and tried to wrap it around his arm. "I just didn't even have the strength in my hands to pull myself to the boat," Don explains. Then, in a nearly tragic twist of fate, the hull of the boat accidentally pushed him underwater. Don was sinking. "I started sliding down toward the center of the boat," he recalls. After all he had been through, it now seemed Don would lose the fight for his life. Suddenly, though, he saw something from the corner of his eye. A hazy golden light appeared at the surface of the water, from off to the left. Don was bewildered. *Where's that coming from? There's no sunshine today.* Then, there was a big splash. Millions of tiny bubbles danced before him and then floated upward. He immediately felt a *strong hand* take hold of his right biceps while a second one grabbed his right forearm. It must be John-T! But who was manning the boat?

Next, *another* set of hands took hold of his left biceps and shoulder blade and they pushed him toward the surface. "I went straight to the ladder," he says, "just like a magnet." *Where*, he wondered, *had John-T found help?* While Don was glad to have made it to the ladder, climbing it was another matter altogether. He was simply too cold and too weak to move. He couldn't even get his foot on the bottom rung. "I just didn't have any strength, and that takes strength even on a good day," he explains.

Again, Don felt strong hands take over. One hand gripped his calf while another one took his ankle. They placed Don's foot on the lowest rung. More hands pressed against his bottom and then propelled him upward. Don recalls, "I went up just like I was on a hydraulic lift. I just stood up. And John-T, who is fifty pounds lighter, flipped me around and dragged me in."

A coast guard helicopter soon whisked Don away, taking him to Jacksonville University, where he remained for four days. He was treated for hypothermia and exhaustion. It wasn't until after a conversation with John-T that Don began coming to terms with the strange events surrounding his rescue.

Recalling the two friends' emotional reunion in his hospital room, Don says, "I just gave John-T the biggest hug going." Smiling at his friend and rescuer, he wondered, *How will I ever be able to express my gratitude?* He remembers thinking, *What do you say to somebody who saves your life? Just "thank you" is not good enough.*

Then on a curious note, Don said, "John-T, you scared me half to death. Why did you jump in the water?"

John-T looked confused. "What are you talking about?"

"Well, I saw you jump in," Don explained, "and you grabbed hold of me."

"Don, what are you talking about?" John-T shot back. "I never left the boat. I pulled you in from the swim platform. And I was alone."

Don sank back into his pillow. He says, "Then it hit me, like a ton of bricks. All the pieces of the puzzle suddenly came together." The *voice* that he heard in the ocean! Now he realized it was the same voice that had told him he was going over the boat. Don Spann believes this to be an encounter of the darkest kind, with the one the Bible calls *the Deceiver.* "As far as I'm concerned, it was the devil himself," he says.

However, the hands that helped rescue Don also served to change his life dramatically. His outlook now is one of trust and faith in God. He believes that it was "the *will* of Jesus for His guardian angels to help me in some way. I don't know why, but they did."

He doesn't think of his ordeal as something negative. "I call it a blessing," he says. "I know I've experienced the hands-on of a guardian angel, and maybe more than one."

THE INVISIBLE FORCE

In 1941, Rodney Kephart found himself in a strange territory of invisible forces. He was caught between two great powers pitted in a historic drama that would soon unfold for him in a most unexpected way.

As a young civilian carpenter, Rodney had been assigned to Wake Island in the South Pacific during the spring of 1941 to work construction. He spent most of that year helping to build a new air base, while across the sea the Empire of the Rising Sun was covertly gathering its powerful flying forces.

On December seventh, Japan struck Pearl Harbor. The war had begun, and the Japanese then turned their sights toward Wake Island. Rodney remembers that day vividly. He was working in the carpenter shop when the attack began. "The first warning we had was the airport exploding and I rushed out onto the back of the platform where I was working. I looked up into the eyes of the Japanese. They were strafing us with fifty-caliber machine guns." Rodney ran for cover, narrowly escaping injury.

Immediately following the attack, Rodney rushed to the hospital to volunteer in caring for the injured in an emergency triage. "That night," he explains, "we ran twenty-one patients through surgery between nine and one in the morning. Everything from amputations to shrapnel removal." It was grueling work.

After an exhausting double shift, Rodney was relieved from work and ordered to get some rest. Wearily, he wandered down the corridor toward a room that had two empty beds. Nearing the room, he was struck by the fact that it was brilliantly illuminated. *What's going on in here?* he wondered.

Curiosity beckoned him as he walked toward the door. Strangely, though, he found he was unable to enter the room. "I just seemed to lose my momentum to go forward," Rodney explains, "and there seemed to be a personal force standing in the doorway to prevent me from entering. I tried three times to enter, and the same thing each time, I just couldn't proceed."

Exhausted and confused, Rodney turned around and walked a half a mile back to his own barracks. He gave no more thought to the bizarre incident . . . until he put it together with what he saw the next morning.

"The Japanese had just raided us again," he says. After the raid was over, Rodney made his way back to the hospital to assess the damage. He was startled by what he saw. "They had dropped an incendiary bomb in the hospital." The hospital was badly burned and the wing where Rodney would have stayed was completely destroyed. It appeared as if the bomb had made a direct hit on the very room he had chosen to sleep in the night before!

Rodney's life was saved that day by the unexplainable force that had prevented him from stepping into the ill-fated room. With a smile, he says, "It's the reason that I'm here today to be able to talk with you. My life was spared by that miracle."

SUPERNATURAL RESCUE

Albert Gorsuch was a typical *good man whose life had gone bad.* Life's former hopes for happiness had eluded him and, during his later years, he became lost on a path of self-destructive behavior. Seeking escape from his dismal future, he turned to alcohol. "I couldn't wait in the morning to start drinking," says Albert, "and then I got into gambling." His life quickly spiraled out of control as drinking, gambling, and secrecy became his main companions. Before long, Albert had virtually gambled away his family's life savings.

His one mainstay, however, was his loving wife, Catherine. "Why this wonderful woman remained with me," recalls Albert, "was totally beyond me." There were many mornings when he stumbled into the kitchen with a hangover, fully expecting some kind of reproach. Instead, he would see her cheerful face, smiling at him despite his obvious weaknesses. "She would be out there getting my breakfast," he recalls. "And she would be *singing* and going on like that, and I would think, *God, how can she do these things? How is it that she can do these things when she knows what I've been doing?"*

His wife's love may have been steadfast, but it wasn't long before his boss had enough. For the previous two years, Albert had been training a younger man to do his kind of work. "One day my boss came up and said, 'Albert, I can't pay the two of you for this job. You're old enough, and I would like you to retire.'" Albert remembers clearly, "That's the day when the earth crashed around me."

Albert knew what he had to do. The only solution he could see to his bleak future was to remove himself from the picture.

Albert describes the scene. "I went out and got in my car and I started down the road. I was crying. I didn't want to commit suicide, but God hadn't answered my prayers. He hadn't helped me in any way." With tears streaming down his face, Albert pleaded with God to save him. "I prayed all the way down the road," he recalls. "And I asked, *God, is there no help for me?* But I never got an answer."

Finally, Albert arrived at his destination, a high bridge. He paused momentarily and then, with a heavy heart, got out of his car. He knew exactly what he had to do. "I started over toward the railing," he says, "and then something, *a force,* just took hold of me." Next, Albert experienced something truly remarkable. "It lifted me up off of my feet and took me back to my car." He had the feeling he was being cradled, completely enfolded by the *wings of a bird.* Full of wonder, he cried out, *"Oh, God, is this an angel?"*

As Albert wept, he heard a comforting voice consoling him, "You will be all right." Time stood still as the presence lovingly assured Albert it would not leave until he calmed down. "It had me like a little baby in its arms," he explains. Soon a gentle peace descended on Albert's weary soul. He was especially moved and encouraged by the parting words from the mysterious voice. *"God isn't done with you yet, son. God isn't done with you yet."*

And then it was over. Alone in his car, Albert reflected on his amazing experience. It was all so wonderful . . . but who would believe such a wild story? Wiping tears from his eyes, Albert prepared to start the car. Looking around, however, Albert realized he was no longer near the bridge. How did he get *here?* His car was on the side of Ivy Mill Road, more than a mile from the bridge where he had originally parked. He had to tell Catherine!

Albert returned home and told his wife everything. He confessed his attempted suicide, and sobbed through his description of what followed. True to her compassionate nature, Catherine believed his story. She thanked God for the miracle that had saved her husband's life. And her gratefulness grew as she watched Albert turn his life around completely and permanently. Today he shares his story whenever possible of how his life was saved by a loving presence sent by God.

CHAPTER 13

Through the Veil

❧

Joan of Arc (1412?–31), called the Maid of Orléans and Maid of France, was seventeen years old when she inspired a French army to break the English siege of the French city of Orléans and to win other important victories. Joan spent much of her time in prayer and was about thirteen when she first saw a heavenly vision. For some time she told no one of the visions.

At her trial for heresy in England, Joan was asked what language her voices spoke: "They speak better French than you!

"The voices say 'Daughter of God, go on, go on, go on! I will be your help. Go on!' When I hear these voices, I feel such great joy that I wish I could always hear it!"

She was condemned to die. Yet she never lost her faith, even when the end came, and she was tied to a stake. As soon as Joan noticed that the fire had been lit, her last words were "My voices did come from God, and everything that I have done was by God's order.

"Hold the crucifix up before my eyes so I may see it until I die.

"Jesus, Jesus, Jesus!"

❧

HERE ARE TIMES when a person's supernatural encounter provides a glimpse of the other side. In the following story, a young woman's extraordinary visit to Heaven during a near-death experience introduces her to someone on *that* side whom she would meet again upon returning to *this* side of the veil—the separation between Heaven and Earth.

By the time she was fourteen, "Sarah" Powell had lived a normal and happy childhood, surrounded by loving parents, a younger sister, and good friends. But life can sometimes turn on a dime, as was about to happen to Sarah. She was about to lose one thing that nobody ever thinks of losing—her *self*. Yet, as we shall see, through one's loss much can be gained.

THE INVISIBLE FRIEND

Sarah lifted her head up from her pillow and somewhat bleary-eyed, looked at the clock on her nightstand. It was a little before nine o'clock in the morning, time to take her medicine . . . Wearily, she sat up in bed. She felt a little better, but she was still not over the cold that had kept her home from school that morning. She staggered downstairs and began unscrewing the medicine bottle when, suddenly, she heard a noise. It sounded like it was coming from the roof. *Oh my God,* she thought. *Someone's trying to break in!*

Terrified, Sarah first tried to dial her mom's workplace, but the line was busy. Next, she raced downstairs. "I checked to see if there were any keys in the house," she says, "but my sister had taken the last set." With all of the deadbolts locked, Sarah realized to her horror that she was a prisoner in her own home. Her mind raced frantically. *What should I do?* She commanded herself, *Think, Sarah, think!* With her heart pounding wildly, she decided to go back upstairs and try to find her parents' gun. *At least I can protect myself,* she reasoned.

Silently, Sarah crept up the steps. "When I got to the hallway upstairs," she says, "I didn't hear anything. I figured that *whoever it was* must have seen me go down the stairs and had left." Much relieved, Sarah went to the window to see if she could see anything; maybe a car pulling away or someone on foot. Nothing. *Oh well,* she thought, breathing a deep sigh of relief. *At least they're gone . . .*

Then suddenly, two men and two women burst out from her walk-in closet. The teenage gang, apparently on drugs, may have planned a simple burglary but, caught off guard, were suddenly confronted by a screaming girl. Sarah was completely helpless to fight off her assailants. One was waving a gun. Sarah explains, "The bigger one, who seemed to be in charge, grabbed a pillow and put it on my head and tried to smother me." She fought for her life, wrestling with her attacker until she freed her face. As her head emerged from beneath the pillow, she found herself looking directly at a very distinctive tattoo on her attacker's arm. "When he realized that I saw that tattoo," she says, "he became enraged and he hit me across the head with his gun and I fell over." Sarah then relates, "That's the point when I think *I must have died.*"

Fear and pain were suddenly behind her. Sarah describes leaving her body and waking beneath a beautiful tree, in what appeared to be a heavenly paradise. "It seemed like the best place that anybody could ever be," she recalls. "This is the place that I would definitely want to spend eternity." She was just getting acquainted with her new surroundings when she looked up to see a figure approaching. "It turned out to be a good friend of mine from school named Brian," she says. Brian had been killed only four days earlier in a terrible automobile accident. He told her that he had come to bring comfort and to explain what was happening to her. "He said that I was going to be okay, and I was going to be spared, for a certain reason. I still had something left to do," she says. He also said that he had someone he wanted her to meet.

Soon after, a tall man in a distinctive white suit appeared to her. She asked his name. He laughed and said, "You wouldn't be able to pronounce it . . . But you can call me George." He had a pleasant British accent, and carried with him a top hat. He said, "I'm going to be with you for a time. I've known you all your life . . . and you may think of me as your *guardian angel.*" Sarah gathered that he was appearing to her in this peculiar outfit for a reason, though she didn't yet understand what it was.

His gentle manner comforted Sarah as he lovingly reassured her that she was going to be all right. He, too, confirmed that it was not yet her time to die; she would have to go back. "He told me I was brought there to rest, and to gain the courage and energy to go on and finish what I was supposed to finish," Sarah says. And then, she recalls, "It seemed like everything started to kind of fade out, and before I knew it, I was back in my room."

As Sarah gradually regained consciousness, she found herself on her bedroom floor, hog-tied. She was looking up into the gentle eyes of her dog as he softly licked her face. "I didn't know where I was, who I was, how I got there, or why I was tied up," she says. The trauma had evidently left Sarah with total amnesia. She noticed immediately, though, that the phone cord was lying across her face. "I pulled the cord with my teeth. The phone fell on the floor and was knocked off the hook." Though too foggy to even remember her own name, Sarah did have the presence of mind to press *redial* on the phone handle with the tip of her tongue. She hoped to contact someone who might know her and come to her rescue. She says, "When I pressed redial, it called my mom's work because that's who I called before the people came in."

Her mother's boss answered the phone and listened carefully as the hysterical young girl described her situation. Sarah relates, "She talked to me and tried to figure out who I was. But she couldn't tell, so she got on the loudspeaker and told all her employees that 'there is a kid on the phone who says she is in a pink bedroom, tied up, and there are a lot of teddy bears around.'" Sarah's mother knew at once that it was her daughter and frantically raced home. She searched the house, which had been completely ransacked, and found Sarah on her bedroom floor with her arms and feet bound by a cord.

Deborah Powell untied her daughter and tried to find out what happened, but Sarah's expression was blank. "She was like a zombie," Deborah recalls. "Sarah was confused and had no memory of her home or family." She was immediately rushed to the hospital, where she was checked and treated for head injuries. Doctors suspected she was suffering from dissociative amnesia, a form of posttraumatic stress disorder. She was eventually sent home and advised simply to rest.

But amnesia is a cunning thief. It takes away the pain, and leaves a person with nothing familiar to hold on to. Sarah's friends, and even her parents, were all strangers. Her once comfortable home was now just someone else's house, a place where she felt she did not belong. Depression settled over her like a heavy shroud. "I lost my life, and I didn't feel like I had anything to live for. I didn't even get to remember the experiences that I'd had before," she says. Her family rallied around her, trying to help her remember her past, but Sarah seemed almost unreachable.

One month after the crime was committed, Sarah collapsed to the floor with what appeared to be a grand mal-type seizure. It was during this and subsequent seizures that the terrifying details of the crime began to return to Sarah's memory. Tortured by these horrifying memories, she withdrew still further from her family and friends. She coped with her pain the best she could, often sitting alone, rocking herself back and forth and singing quietly.

During this time, a therapist named Sharon began making regular visits to the Powells' home, trying to help their daughter regain her memory. Sharon became the one person that Sarah felt comfortable enough to talk to. Their sessions together were often emotional as Sarah dealt with the painful memories. One day, immediately following a terrible seizure, Sharon called by chance to talk with Sarah. They had been talking for just a few minutes when, Sarah recalls, "While I was talking to Sharon, a *light* appeared before me. At first, it was a circular shape and then it came down to be a long oval. And it was . . . well, I knew that it was the one I had met under the tree when I died! It was George. I immediately stopped crying, and Sharon, the psychologist, just seemed amazed. She said, 'Why did you calm down so quickly?' And I said, 'Well, George says I'm going to be okay. *He's* gonna take care of me now.'" The therapist did not know what to think as Sarah explained her vague memories of the near-death experience.

"In the next few minutes I was laughing," Sarah says. "I just completely forgot about any worries I had." George was reminding Sarah that she needed to check on her sister, Helen, who had been frightened by the sight of the horrible seizure. Sarah agreed and went downstairs to find her sister.

As she entered the living room, she found Helen sobbing quietly on the couch. Sarah sat on the coffee table and looked deeply into her sister's eyes. Helen was overcome with emotion. The longer she looked at Sarah, the more she cried. Sarah then calmly asked her sister to put her hand over a certain place on the couch. Without further explanation, Sarah was guiding her sister's hand to touch the angel, which only she could see. "I didn't know why, but I did it," Helen admits. "And at that moment, I just felt peace. It was just one of the most wonderful feelings I've ever had."

From the sideline, their mother, Deborah, was watching the scene in utter amazement. "I'm sure my mom was puzzled," Helen reflects.

Next, Sarah invited her mother to sit down. She calmly informed her, "Mom, I have a guardian angel, and he's gonna be with me for a while. He's gonna help us get through this."

A little shocked, but wanting to support her daughter's positive new outlook, Deborah replied, "Well, okay . . ."

Sarah's father, Mark, joined them in the living room and was told about "the angel." Sarah continued, "He says he's been with me for a long time, since I was a baby." Taking a deep breath, Sarah looked directly at her mother and went on. "Well, he says to tell you that when I was a little kid I used to laugh at him because he had this big hat that he always pushed away from his eyes."

Deborah looked at her husband and immediately burst into tears as memories of her daughter's early childhood flooded her mind. In amazement, Mark nodded as Deborah proceeded to remind Sarah about specific scenes from her youth. She remembered that during the years when Sarah was two and three, Sarah would break into little bursts of laughter for no apparent reason. Deborah fondly recalls, "We'd peek in your room and say, 'What are you laughing at?' In a giggly voice, you would reply, 'Umm, the man with the big hat comes and makes me laugh.'" Deborah had even saved some of the pictures that Sarah frequently drew of this man in the white tux and top hat. Deborah today admits, "We were just floored by what was happening to our grown daughter."

Later that night, when Deborah reflected back on the evening's events, she began to accept that something undeniably spiritual was going on. And over the coming months, the mysterious presence, who became affectionately known in the Powells' home simply as *George*, helped to bring about Sarah's emotional healing. Memories and details of Sarah's life returned to her gradually. She also began to remember, little by little, the trauma of the dreadful assault, and with each stage of painful recovery she would be comforted by her invisible friend.

When she was fully recovered, Sarah was told by her messenger-helper that the visits would have to end. She wrote his parting words into a note-book, realizing that she may never see him again in her lifetime. Among other encouraging words he gave her, she was told, "You have proven to be strong, and your family as well. I know you can get through this, and when you do, you'll come out even more strong than before."

The impact of the experience on the whole Powell family was profound. It brought them all closer to God, and to one another. Each of them radiated peace and gratitude, while they spoke with me during our interviews, about the answer they received in their time of helplessness. When I asked Mark Powell how he felt about the stranger who visited their home during the recovery of his daughter, he replied, "I have to thank him, as I have to thank God, that he did for Sarah so many things that, for a time, I could not do."

While interviewing Joan Wester Anderson for the *Angel Stories* program, we talked about children. Joan wrote an inspiring book called *An Angel to Watch Over Me*, which contains stories of children's encounters with angels. Joan says:

"I think we've probably always known intellectually that children have an innate spirituality, but it wasn't brought home to me until recently, when I began getting these letters, and I was just in awe of what was being described. And that's how I began to hear stories about *imaginary friends*. Now, pediatricians have known for years that children create these things. They need a friend because they're lonely, because their older brothers and sisters have gone to school and so they'll have somebody named 'Margie' who will come and sit at the dinner table with them. And everyone kind of patiently pats them on the head and thinks, *Well, this will be over as soon as they get older.* And it *will* be over soon, but I think that the Margies might actually be angels that are with them for a time. And then, as that veil between Heaven and Earth begins to descend, farther and farther down, and as the children get older and move farther and farther away from their heavenly roots, they don't see these things anymore. They were bringing something of Heaven to Earth for a short period."

A MISTY CLOUD

We hear countless stories of angels who warn or rescue people in their time of need. But I also found stories of angels tending to another kind of need—the deep need for comfort that people face when grieving the loss of someone dear to them.

I was introduced to Scott Degenhardt by an author named John Ronner, who wrote *Do You Have a Guardian Angel?* and other books about angels. Scott spearheaded a group called the *Organization of Near-Death Survivors*, which meets once a month in Murfreesboro, Tennessee, to share personal stories from people who have had a close brush with death. Scott's story *is not* about his own NDE. Instead, it is what he calls a *shared-death experience* that happened the night his father died.

Degenhardt describes his relationship with his father as the modern-day version of "The Prodigal Son." Scott had become estranged from the family during his turbulent teenage years, and didn't communicate with them very much throughout most of his twenties. Then one day, Scott got the news that his father had terminal cancer. That was when Scott Degenhardt decided to put away the past and reconcile with his family.

"I spent the last three months of my father's life with him. And we became very, very close. There were many nights when he would ask me to come over and just be with him at night."

The healing of their relationship had a price, and the bond that grew between father and son meant a deep sharing of both joy and terrible suffering.

"He was in extreme pain, because the cancer had just run through his entire body," recalls Scott. The terrible wait was agonizing for the whole family, and everyone knew that the end was near. But exactly when death would arrive was anyone's guess.

"Then one night," says Scott, "I was in bed, mulling over the day's activities and feelings, and trying to process how I was going to react whenever I would finally get the word that my father had died. It certainly wouldn't be a surprise because we knew that it was just a matter of *any minute now*. And I sort of went through those feelings and emotions right before I drifted off to sleep."

Scott remembers what happened next. "I was awakened by this *spirit* that zoomed right over from my feet, right over the top of me, and hovered on the left side of my bed at my shoulders. The best way to describe it is sort of a glowing, misty cloud. But I immediately recognized it as my father."

Scott says that he then lay absolutely still. He was not at all frightened but rather excited by the idea that his father was finally liberated from the body. And he *felt* the sensations that his father was undergoing. "He was emanating these absolute feelings of well-being and joy and freedom. While my father was hovering beside my bed, we were just sort of basking in each other's presence, feeling each other's feelings."

And then Scott shared what most people only describe from *their own* near-death experience. "The best way to describe it is a connection opened up off into the distance. I could feel an *awareness* of a far-off place. I could hear other beings talking among themselves. They were what I would describe as *angels*.

"My father turned and looked in that direction, and then he looked back at me. He acknowledged them, and immediately said to me, 'They're calling me now, and I have to go.' And when my father said it, there was more . . . There was this complete sense of mission and understanding of where he had to go next. That he had to go with these beings and it was time for him to proceed on to the next realm that awaited him."

In the morning, Scott's phone rang. It was his mother calling to break the news. "I know, Mom," Scott told her. It was a while before he was able to fully share with anyone what had happened that night.

Hearing Scott's story gave me a sense of inspiration, and at the same time a deep feeling of comfort. Anyone who has ever lost a parent knows that, at that instant, our entire life up to that point comes to a crossroads. No matter what the relationship was like, positive or negative, we understand deep inside that the flame of one who sparked our own life has gone out. Yet we know that the flame still burns—at least inside of us—and, we hope, somewhere else as well.

I went through an amazing growth during the time when my own father passed on. It became a point of departure in my adult life, not unlike the passage from boyhood into manhood, from receiver to provider. The passing of the patriarchal (or matriarchal) torch in the relay of life is a mystical transformation that affects us in deeply spiritual ways. I wish for everyone who goes through it that the experience of a parent's death will be as extraordinary an episode in the epic life journey as was the crossing over of my dear father, Houstin Shockey.

PART THREE

The Afterlife

The Call

WAS SHOCKED when I got that phone call, the one that nobody ever wants, or really ever expects to get. My mother explained that my dad was fighting for every breath of life, and the doctors didn't offer much hope. Even though we live six hundred miles apart and only saw each other on holidays, at least we were on the same *planet* and could pick up the phone and say "hello." The likelihood of losing all that seemed almost impossible to grasp.

My father had become one of my best friends, and certainly one of my most faithful. He had been there to pull me out of the riptide at the beach in Santa Monica when I was six. He was there to listen to me talk endlessly about my adolescent problems concerning girls, self-image, and career decisions. He came to be with me, to hug and cry with me, during my divorce from my first wife, Suzanne. And he offered his shoulder a little while later, when I received news that Suzy had died suddenly during the birth of her first child. Now my "rock" needed help. I felt he needed *my* help . . . but what could I do?

Houstin Shockey was a strong and handsome man, even at eighty-seven years old. He was the son of a successful lawyer, and having come from a long line of lawyers, became one himself. But he didn't enjoy law much, and advised me to follow my interests in filmmaking. He once told me he wished he had followed his own fascination for physics, where one's mind could explore life beyond the confines of man's law. He realized the limitations of the logical mind.

He used to say, "Nobody can 'logically' convince me of the existence of God or the supernatural, because a good lawyer can always conjure up an even more persuasive logical argument against anything, including the Divine."

He said, "If there is indeed a spiritual reality, it must exist on a separate level of existence than anything we can understand with our limited brain-power."

Several years earlier, at the ripe age of seventy, it hadn't been logic or reasoning that finally touched him, but a simple heartfelt prayer that was answered in a supernatural way. He had been taken to a healing service and, much to his own surprise, was healed of a painful deteriorating hip that had been tormenting him for years. In his own way of thinking, the physical heal-ing was not the focus of the "miracle," but that it opened the door to his *believing*.

It was quite inspiring to see Dad go through the changes he made in the last seventeen years of his life. He became joyous, and was eternally grateful for everything around him, especially for my mother, who had discovered her own spiritual life several years earlier.

Now it seemed my father may be leaving us soon, and I didn't know if my tears were for him, or for *us* who would no longer be able to enjoy his com-pany. Mom said the doctors predicted he would live for several more months, and I had already planned with my wife to take a trip to my parents' home in Annapolis the following week for Easter. Still, I wanted to do something immediate to share my feelings with Dad, but he was too weak for phone calls.

So I decided there was only one thing that I could do. I would write him a letter.

When I began writing, I really didn't know how to start:

> *Dear Dad,*
> *I'm so sorry to hear what you're going through. I know you're rugged, but you gave us a good scare . . .*

Lord, I thought, *is this about my fears?* I crumpled up the page. And then it slowly came. It settled into my heart like a gentle rain.

> *Dear Dad,*
> *I'm writing you this letter because I don't know if I'll ever see you again, yet I have so much I want to say. Dad, several years ago when I was still grieving over the death of Suzanne, I found a great deal of comfort in some books I was reading—about dying. It was at that time that I met a doctor of psychiatry, a researcher named Dr. Raymond Moody. I'm sending a copy of a book that he wrote, which was a great deal of help to me then. Dr. Moody has observed a pattern that occurs in people the world over, regardless of their cultural backgrounds. It's about his research into the stories of people who have approached death, many of whom actually had the experience of dying and then were revived to tell about it . . .*

I had recently met the author whose research in the field of *near-death experiences* had been a great inspiration during the early years of my career as a special-effects filmmaker (as mentioned earlier, it was upon reading his book *Life After Life* in college that I patterned my senior film project on the visionary accounts of the tunnel and the light, which pioneered my first efforts into film effects).

I had been told by a friend that this particular author was visiting Nashville to do a radio talk show, so I called his hotel and asked if we could meet and chat over breakfast. I fully expected to meet a stuffy old doctor of psychiatry whose interest in death had left him with a glum personality. Instead, I was greeted in the lobby by an unpretentious character with a quick wit and an enthusiasm for life.

Over breakfast, Dr. Moody colorfully described the phenomenal stories he had gathered in the twenty years that he had been studying the near-death experience. Raymond recounted a sort of composite sketch of the experience—a collage, or montage, of typical elements from the stories he had gathered from over three thousand people who had been clinically dead, and then were resuscitated. I made mental notes. By the time breakfast was over, my cinematic mind's eye was reeling with images of iridescent tunnels, floating out-of-body experiences, and the brilliant light . . . the kinds of things I had been trained to depict in my twelve years as a special-effects filmmaker!

Something else happened that morning that would change the course of my life. Before we said good-bye, I felt compelled to ask Raymond to pray with me. I wasn't sure how Dr. Moody would respond to such a request from someone he just met, but he was ready and willing (I later discovered that his great-uncle was the founder of Moody Bible Institute, who himself had an extraordinary deathbed experience). We prayed, *"If there is a way to make a film about near-death experiences in a way that can help people, would You please show us the way to do it?"*

We also agreed in our prayer that if we did make the film, it should be approached as a creative *work of art* capable of touching the heart, and not just as an academic treatment.

∾

It now occurred to me that my interest in this subject was perhaps going to serve a much greater purpose than I had ever envisioned . . .

My father didn't need an academic lecture from the letter I was writing. Once again I prayed that the stories I had heard would bring comfort to the heart of the one I loved so much.

So I continued to write my last letter to the man who had helped me through the most difficult transitions in my life. Perhaps in some way, I hoped, this would provide some help to him in the transition he was about to make.

CHAPTER 15

Beginning at Life's End

∽

CONTINUED TO WRITE.

I think it was when I heard you were beginning to use an oxygen tank that it really hit home: My father is a mortal man after all (despite what I believed as a child). I also think that with all my reading about the "near-death experience," I am more ready to face death—whether it's mine or yours—without fear. There would be lots of grief and sadness, of course, but I think it's more the kind of sadness we feel as children when a best friend moves away, and you know you won't be seeing them for a long time . . . All the accounts we hear from people who have been revived from the brink of death confirm what our religious traditions tell us about eternal life!

Of course, I didn't go into as much detail in my letter to Dad as I am able to go into now. There were some things we shared that went without saying, but are worth mentioning here so that you can know the nature of our father-son relationship.

We were, by the time I wrote my letter, accustomed to talking straightforwardly about spiritual ideas and particularly about the teachings of Jesus. My father had crossed the bridge of faith more than fifteen years earlier and had became a devout believer in the power of the Spirit.

I clearly remember the night when we first talked about each other's religious beliefs. I was eighteen and he had asked me to join him on an impromptu vacation, which I think he badly needed. We took off with less than a day's planning for a weeklong canoe trip in the Adirondacks, just the two of us. All of the third day had been spent paddling through glistening lakes and winding swamps. Twice that day we had portaged our canoe and camping gear through miles of overgrown footpaths, leaving our muscles cramped and twisted. Twilight came early with dark thunderclouds. We lost the race to pitch camp before rainfall, and crawled into our musty pup tent looking like wet but happy otters. What sticks most in my memory is the comical image of us two hungry campers eating cold hot dogs and mustard in a damp tent, only to discover that we had pitched camp in a soon-to-be raging ravine. So, after adjusting our campsite, we returned to our soaking sleeping bags and tried to make the most of a difficult time.

Maybe it took ripping away civilization like that and getting down to life's basic needs that opened up our conversation. Perhaps it was the great bonding experience we were having that caused him to ask me what I really believed in—what was really important to me. I knew that he was really listening and interested when I told him about the nuggets of gold I had found in Christ's teachings about love, hope, and prayer. It was a real thrill, despite the chilly scenario to share these treasures with my dad, reading from a paperback Bible by the beam of our only dry flashlight. It would be another two years before Dad had his own profound healing experience, but he later told me that our campside chat had touched something in his heart.

I think it is one thing to contemplate death and eternal life while young and healthy—and quite something else when you are standing at death's door. I knew Dad would relate to the stories I was now about to share, hearing them with his heart and with his mind.

They say that at first you may not realize the soul has actually left the body. Some people seem surprised at looking across the room and seeing someone lying "over there," then recognizing it to be themselves—the one they've always known from the mirror!

They may watch family members or doctors making a fuss over their newly vacated body and may even try comforting or reassuring the grieving family members, but nobody seems to hear.

This may seem frustrating, to talk and not be heard, but what happens next is so wonderful that people seem to cope quickly with this new circumstance. The "out of body" state, as they call it, allows free movement that is said to be very enjoyable— floating, moving through objects, and traveling at unlimited speeds and distances at will.

PROOF OF THE SOUL

The initial out-of-body condition is the most commonly reported element of the near-death experience. Generally, it seems that the longer a person is "clinically dead," the more elements they may undergo. Those who revive quickly might not have proceeded through the tunnel to the light, and beyond. So it figures statistically that more stories are told about seeing one's body from a disembodied perspective. To the skeptic, this experience might offer some compelling evidence of the soul's existence apart from the body.

Raymond told me of a woman named Kim who worked at a medical university out West. Kim was involved in resuscitating a young patient named Maria, who had been clinically dead but was successfully revived. When the patient came back to consciousness, Kim was standing by Maria's bedside. Maria grabbed on to Kim and said that during the resuscitation she had traveled out of her body and drifted outside the hospital. She had found herself in midair above the building and saw an *old shoe* on a ledge of a window outside an upper floor of the hospital. Kim's curiosity was aroused enough to check out Maria's bizarre certainty about the shoe. She was shocked when she was able to go there and verify that the shoe was there exactly as the patient had described, but in a place that she could not have known about from her bodily perspective.

Once I began to discuss these out-of-body episodes openly, I discovered many firsthand accounts from people whom I knew: friends, relatives, and acquaintances. For example, I was chatting one evening with the father-in-law of my cousin, when we got onto the subject of NDEs. He took me aside and described something that had happened to him during WWII, something that he obviously hadn't shared with many people.

"I was in the army, serving in Europe," he explained. "The transport ship we were on had been torpedoed and sank quickly, before any of us could prepare the lifeboats.

"In the chaos of wreckage and waves, I held up one other fellow as long as I could. Then, I couldn't help him anymore—the icy water made my arm useless and I just had to let go . . .

"All of my shipmates were lost," he choked, "and I found myself floating alone in the ocean, clinging to a piece of debris.

"I was fighting for my life, and it looked hopeless. I was sure I was going to die," he continued, "when suddenly I saw myself from high above!

"I know I wasn't hallucinating this, but I was up in the air maybe fifty feet above the open seas and could see myself bobbing around down there, struggling to survive."

Then, his strength draining away, he saw himself going under. He remembers praying, "Please, God . . ."

Immediately he found himself beside his wife, who was back in the States.

"When I saw her there alone I realized that I had to stay alive. I couldn't stand the thought of leaving her alone as a war widow."

He managed to stay afloat just a little while longer, long enough for a rescue vessel, which had been tracing the wreckage, to find him, barely alive.

Another acquaintance, the manager for country music singer Garth Brooks, shared her experience from college days. Pam Lewis had been working during the summer in a national park when she was stung by a bee.

"This wasn't a typical bee sting because I quickly realized that there was a problem and I tried to call someone for help," she recalls. "The rest of the ranger stations were about three miles in, and I tried to telephone my boss to send some help when I fell and went unconscious."

Her allergic reaction to the bee sting flung her system into anaphylactic shock, causing her heart to beat erratically.

"Luckily, from what I understand, my boss drove through a little while later and noticed that I would normally wave to him as he came by. But I was lying down on the floor and he called the ambulance."

While Pam was clinging to life, waiting for medical help, she found herself up above the scene, looking down on her body.

"It looked like this sort of feeble, sick person and it didn't dawn on me until it seemed like many minutes later, though I'm sure it was a flash, that the person was me! And they were trying to revive me because I was dying and, in fact, my heart had stopped."

Again and again I have heard that familiar scenario, and I'm sure that anyone who inquires among their own circle of friends would uncover similar reports. The perception of sight, sound, smell, and much more, does seem to exist apart from our physical bodies, and is a powerful piece of evidence pointing to the existence of an eternal soul.

Dad, before I tell you about a most adventurous kind of out-of-body traveling, I want you to promise that you'll come to visit me and say good-bye before you actually leave this world . . . There are occasional reports from people who experienced another dramatic form of traveling—that they actually leave their body, zoom up above the Earth, and travel far into space and see the earth down below.

Dr. Carl Jung experienced this phenomenon when he had a near-death experience in 1944 during a heart attack.

At the beginning of 1944 I broke my foot and this misadventure was followed by a heart attack. Extremely strange things began to happen to me. It seemed to me that I was high up in space. Far below I saw the globe of the Earth bathed in a gloriously blue light. I saw the deep blue sea and the continents. I could see the snow covered Himalayas. I knew that I was at the point of departing from the Earth. The sight of the Earth from this height was the most glorious thing I had ever seen.

ANGELIC HELP

Very often people become aware that they are not alone in this spiritual realm. Many speak about encountering what they refer to as angelic guardians, sometimes referred to as "beings of light," who emanate peace and reassurance and who put the dying person at ease. These angelic helpers seem to be there to help the departed proceed on into the Light, which is distinctly different from—and much more brilliant than—these radiant beings.

"I was suddenly looking at this *light* that seemed to be in the corner of the room," Sandi Rogers, who had a near-death experience in 1976, explains, "but the first thing I thought was, *Where did you come from?* And she said, 'I've always been here, but you weren't able to see me before.' The reason I say 'she' is because she emanated feelings of selflessness—love, all consuming love, understanding, kindness—and those were attributes that I thought of as being feminine."

When hearing stories of NDEs, there is sometimes a confusing distinction between references to *the light* of an angelic being, and *the Light* of the Ultimate Being whom they encounter later. I confess that I misunderstood the identity in Sandi's description of this feminine "light" until several years later when I asked her to set the record straight. The light she referred to was actually what she termed a guardian angel, who *then* brought the woman into the presence of a much larger Light. I think it's an important detail to mention these days, especially when many people seem to put angels in the same rank as God himself.

I continued my description to Dad:

> *. . . Anyway, that's only a starting point because soon, we're told, one becomes aware of a tunnel, which is long and dark and seems to have a brilliant light at the far end.*

THE TUNNEL

The tunnel is sometimes described as a spiraling whirlpool shape with the far end narrower than the opening. It is dark and not very wide. We hear words like "rush" and "swoosh" to describe the sensation of speed one feels while accelerating through this enclosure.

"The next thing I remember," describes one man, "is that I heard a set of chimes . . . and as I looked at an angle, probably thirty-five or forty degrees, I could see a tunnel. The tunnel was like a spiral, like it was moving whether I was moving or not. Then I began to whisk down it, and I could hear these chimes, but I was in utter peace and utter tranquillity and it was such a stark, dramatic difference between what was happening to that body and this place I was—this utter peace."

And another woman says, "I don't know exactly how I entered the tunnel or just at what point, but it was when the guides had asked me if I was ready to leave, and I said, 'Yes.' I felt myself going in an upward motion. The tunnel is not too big, just enough room for one person to go at a time. It doesn't touch you and I didn't reach out and touch the walls, but it's black and I felt myself going up and looking at light—*bright light at the end of the tunnel.*"

THE CHOICE OF LIGHT OR DARKNESS

Although we seem to hear many more stories involving light and love and positive feelings, there are other reports of realms that are not so wonderful. From what I gather, we seem to be faced with similar decisions in the afterlife that we have been faced with all of our earthly lives. The key to where we spend eternity seems to be our own decision, made of our own free will, whether or not to proceed into God's presence—into "the Kingdom of Light," as Paul called it in Colossians 1:12.

Many people have reported witnessing a realm that has become nicknamed "the gray area." Souls who have departed their earthly lives are seen to be there milling about aimlessly, without purpose or direction. Witnesses to this area get the feeling that these colorless spirits are those who could not escape their wordly attachments. Those addicted to drugs, alcohol, sex, food, money, or other earthly compulsions; in other words, those who have *stored their treasures up on Earth* and are unable to let go of them upon death.

An odd feature about this gray area is that the bright light of God is always visible, but those residing in this shadowy realm are completely unaware of it. They are either too self-absorbed, or just too afraid of having their weakness exposed. Some seem to be afraid of the wrath from whom they have been brought up to believe is a God who will not forgive them for their ways.

There are reports of an even more diabolical realm than the gray area, and we will hear about that in more detail in a later chapter.

A fascinating footnote here is that those who are receptive to the Light are drawn into it very quickly. One person reported, "And next . . . as I'm going along I see the gray area, but I did not stop to go in or see just what was going on. I went on to come out into this beautiful pasture, a valleyland with flowers, bright beautiful light and brilliant color—nothing here on Earth is like it at all."

The Light

ONTINUING ON:

It seems that our attraction and desire to be with that Light pulls us faster and faster through the tunnel. The Light at the end is actually a presence, or being, whom I've heard many identify as the "Christ," or "the Light of God." He is personally welcoming us home and fills us with such love, peace, and joy that people seem to have a hard time expressing it fully. I get the impression that He is very informal and friendly, and just glad to see us—like you are with me when I come home for Christmas. (Maybe that's why I've always found the term "Heavenly Father" easy to grasp . . .)

The most compelling links between the Light reported in the NDE and the one we read about in the Scriptures are the qualities of love and forgiveness.

One man from South Carolina described the sense of security he felt while in its presence. "As I moved closer to the Light, I kept being surrounded and filled with this love . . . I can't describe it, except when you haven't seen your parents in a long time—if you've been away from your family and when you first see your Mom and your Dad, that feeling you get as a small kid. I knew I was safe. I knew everything was peaceful, and I knew it was right."

An elderly woman echoes this report of parental compassion. "This is the most wonderful part of it. It is a warm, loving light. It's very masculine, but it also has overtones of motherly love and sisterly love. This just pulsates around. He has totally accepted me and forgiven me for everything I've ever done, but the question is, can I forgive myself for some of these selfish things I have done?"

One straightforward identification of this light came from a gentleman who had died and was revived back in 1943, long before people had heard the term "near-death experience": "And sitting there, I was wondering what to do next when suddenly that room became flooded with light and then three things happened simultaneously, just like that," he says, snapping his fingers. "Something deep inside of my spiritual being, which was sitting on the side of the bed (and was looking at my corpse lying *in* the bed) was told to 'Stand up, you're in the presence of *the Son of God.*' Out of that light stepped the most amazing being I have ever been in the presence of . . . the most power-fully built male I have ever seen."

After mentally processing all the NDE accounts I have heard, I have no doubt who it is we face when we die. I also believe that many people will be surprised by the depth of His love and the extent of His forgiveness.

This is the part that is so amazing it always "blows my mind" to think about . . .
I hope my description can do it justice, because this seems to contain the answer to
the meaning of life, death, and love!

While we are in the midst of this all-loving, all-forgiving brilliant light of God,
He takes us on a grand-tour review of our entire life, down to the slightest detail!
Now, Dad, from what I've gathered by these reports, it is not like a fast-motion
movie, which would be hard to digest in an instant. Instead (and try to use your
expanded grasp of physics to envision this) it seems to be some kind of multidimen-

sional time matrix . . . Compare it to many strings of pearls crisscrossing through infinite space. Each point, or pearl, is a moment of time, and each string of moments represents a personal relationship, or one's family life, or the progression of one's career. And here's where it gets really interesting. We witness these things all at once, no longer measured by a linear time scale. Through this "Big Picture" we can immediately see the cause & effect of all our actions on those people in our life—and vice versa—theirs on us. Like ripples in a pond, we can see how our life has intersected with the lives of others. And get this (if you can believe it): We can empathetically feel those other people's perceptions and emotions as if we were them, while simultaneously reliving our own memory from our own point of view!!!

But as if that weren't amazing enough, there seems to be a grand purpose to this epic rerun. It seems that while we are watching this emotion-filled life review, we are being cleansed, by the Light, with a sense of forgiveness for all those things we see and may feel remorseful about. And here seems to be the purpose behind the whole experience. While we are being bathed in this unconditional love, compassion, forgiveness, and empathy, we are being asked one recurring question, telepathically (which of course can only be answered openly and honestly). Essentially that question is, "In your life, have you learned to love in the way that I love?" Or perhaps put another way, "When you were limited to your earthly perceptions, did you share love, forgiveness, and compassion in the ways that you experience with me now?"

JUDGE NOT . . .

During this "life review," as many have called it, one honestly and fairly evaluates one's own life for the purpose of learning from his or her experiences.

As one person interviewed said, "I had a panoramic view of my life, every feeling, every thought, every action, every deed, all at the same time. And as it started happening, I began to see how I affected the person that I had an encounter with, and then how it affected those *one step removed* from us and how *they in turn* were affected. And believe me, there is nothing hidden in your life."

We see the positive effects: "You will see the things that you did out of your heart—helping an old woman, picking a kid up, helping someone—an action that you take uncalculated, unthought, just out of the goodness of your heart. These things herald through the universe. Not your great accomplishments. Not what you achieved or what you *think* has value. The little things have value."

We see our misplaced priorities, as one woman humbly admits. "What I'd always thought were important and nice things I had done, they didn't even count for anything. It's the little, unknown things that you do for one another that count—helping to give others love and a helping hand along the way—and at the same time you're benefiting because you're receiving also."

The Light shines into every cubbyhole of our existence and, like a good teacher, asks us to evaluate ourselves.

"And when you look at it," recounts one man, "you look at it from a place to review. And to be critical of yourself, not be judged or be condemned. There was no condemnation in it. There was none. There was nothing but 'Hey look at yourself . . . look at who you really are.' And to look at what you've done and then give it a value, in the eyes of God."

"And the question was," summarizes another, "'What have you *done with your life?*' Well, I'm looking around this panoramic view, and I'm hoping that He'll notice some good things and, of course, I'm trying to pick the best things and hoping He wouldn't see some rather embarrassing things that happened to me as a teenager. And I thought, 'Well, I was an *Eagle Scout . . .*' Immediately He responded, 'That glorified *you.*' The question came the second time, 'What have you done with your life to *show Me?*' And this time the emphasis was on '*show*

Me.' But I understood what he was saying. He was asking me if I had learned to love my fellow human beings the way that He totally accepted and loved me."

These scenes leave me with some profound conclusions about the dynamics of *love*. They all seem to contain the essential quality of the Greatest Commandment: *Love God with all your heart and with all your soul and with all your mind . . . and Love your neighbor as yourself.* Several other teachings of Jesus seem to mirror the concept that *loving others might just be a smart investment.*

If we are going to one day find ourselves in a position to *feel* the effects of our actions on other people, as if we *were* them, then shouldn't we be loving others as if *they were ourselves? What you do unto the least of these My brothers you do unto Me";* "*Do unto others as you would have them do unto you*"; "*Judge not lest you be judged.*" These ideas reflect how connected we all are. The human tendency is to fall short of these ideals, and might seem to add up to a formula for judging ourselves unworthy of ever being in God's Kingdom. The *good news* is that the Lord loves us and forgives us in spite of everything.

> *Now, Dad, I know this is going to sound incredible, but something just happened as I was sitting here trying to figure out how to end this letter . . . The doorbell rang and who do you suppose it was? Two young ladies, a teenage girl and her older cousin, were going door to door handing out religious literature. The older one, perhaps in her mid-twenties, was a lovely girl (whom I suspect may have been an angel) and she shared two Bible verses with me. I explained that I only had a minute to spare, but the lines she read cut right to my heart, making me cry right there on the doorstep (can you imagine that?). It was so beautifully delivered, and so perfectly timed, that I want to write them down now, since they were obviously intended by God to be included in your letter:*
>
> *2 Peter 3:13—"But in keeping with His promise we are looking forward to a new heaven and a new earth, the home of righteousness"; and,*

Revelation 21:3&4—"*And I heard a loud voice from the throne saying, 'Now the dwelling of God is with men, and he will be with them and He will be their God. He will wipe away every tear from their eyes. There will be no more death or mourning, or crying or pain, for the old order of things has passed away.'*"

Dad, I promise I'm not inventing that story—it's exactly what happened, and that message is a perfect way to sum up this letter. There's really a lot more I want to say to you, but Stowe and I will be home for Easter, which is ten days from today, so we'll talk more then.

As for this long essay on our entry into Heaven, you may not witness it yourself for years . . . only God knows the length of our days. Life is unpredictable and, who knows, I may get there before you do. But whatever happens, I want you to know that I feel very blessed to have had you as my father, and I love you very much.

With great love & respect,

Peter

We went home for Easter and had a wonderful time. Though it was difficult to see Dad confined to his bed with an oxygen mask, we spent several memorable days together. We often did nothing more than just look into each other's eyes. I could tell that he was ready, like someone prepared for a long journey . . . or adventure. And then, after saying our good-byes, Stowe and I returned to our home in Nashville.

Mom says that Dad asked her to read the letter to him several more times, and that it brought him encouragement as they talked about it. I don't really know what he was thinking about during those last days, in his quiet moments of preparation. Thinking back. Looking ahead. Perhaps one day I will know.

It was about three weeks later when we got the phone call. I was told that he died with a smile on his face, and the last words he said were, *"The Light . . ."*

Who's Dead?

T TOOK ABOUT A YEAR to raise the financing to produce the film *Life After Life*, but we finally did. While scripting the film, it dawned on me that the letter to my father would be a very good way to open the story. Although it was an intimately personal letter, I found that people who read it were moved by it. Ultimately, it became the answer to our prayer about making a film that would touch people's hearts. Somehow it seemed fitting that the letter introducing my father to the stories of near-death experiences would become the vehicle to introduce viewers to those inspiring stories. In this chapter you will hear the full experience of Viola Horton, one of those whom we interviewed at length.

I met Viola Horton on a beautiful spring day in 1991, twenty years after her amazing near-death experience. She cheerfully agreed to fly up to Nashville from Augusta, Georgia, where she and her husband, Jud, lived. She would be among several people whom Raymond Moody had suggested we interview for the film.

Viola impressed me as a really sweet soul—a kind of country grandmother. In fact, I wished she had been my own grandmother! The wisdom she had gained from her years here on Earth plus the knowledge she acquired from her close encounter with death would have been nice to be around while growing up. She had a good sense of humor, too, which put me and my film crew at ease as we anxiously prepared for the shoot that day.

The original plan was for Dr. Moody to sit next to the cameraman and have Viola address him while she was being filmed. It didn't take too long, though, before she was being "interviewed" by everyone in the room, which included the film crew, my wife, and a few friendly neighbors who happened to drop by. Her story and the way she told it was heartwarming.

It all began when Viola was admitted into an Augusta, Georgia, hospital in the spring of 1971 for routine gallbladder surgery. The operation was believed to have been successful. Not wanting to become dependent on pain medications, Viola refused all drugs after the third day. As she would soon learn, though, she was *not* on the road to recovery. She suffered for the following three days as her pain intensified. Her condition worsened, and on May fifth at 12:15 P.M. Viola died on the operating table. This was the start of her amazing journey.

WHO'S GONE?

The doctor looked up at the nurse, then, taking a heavy breath, solemnly cast his eyes down toward a woman lying motionless on the operating table. The surgical room, which just moments earlier had echoed with the doctor's desperate attempts to resuscitate the woman, was now completely still. Only the steady tone of a flat-lining heart monitor broke the silence—a painful reminder of the scene that had just unfolded. The time of death was duly noted. As far as they could tell, their efforts to save the life of Viola Horton had failed.

"I've lost her," the doctor sighed. "She's gone . . . she's dead."

Well, who's he talking about? Who's gone? wondered Viola. She was in excruciating pain when she heard a faint buzzing in her ear and then felt herself "pop" out of her body. Free of her earthly shell, she immediately went to the head of the bed where she "sat down" to have a look around, and then found herself floating up to the ceiling, hovering over her now lifeless body. A new sense of freedom swept over her. She suddenly felt strangely unfettered by the usual labels with which she had always identified herself. For the moment, she was no one's wife, mother, or daughter. And for a woman who had just been pronounced dead, *why, she had never felt more alive! But how could this be?* she wondered.

Viola observed the doctors momentarily and then glanced about the operating room. As she did so, she became aware of voices—people out in the hallway. The room had been completely sealed off for surgery, but as Viola would soon discover, walls and closed doors presented no obstacle to her. She simply went *through* them, like vapor through a screen door.

She encountered her anxious family in the hall. She noticed right away that her daughter, Kathy, was wearing an outfit that Viola considered unbecoming. Upset and in a hurry, Kathy had apparently left home in a rush. She had grabbed whatever clothes she could find and, in a strangely mismatched outfit, dashed to the hospital. Shocked that her daughter was dressed this way in public, Viola immediately went to her and said, "Kathy, go home and change your clothes." Kathy did not respond to her mother. It seemed that Kathy was unable to hear her. Never one to give up, though, Viola persevered, urging her husband, "Jud, take Kathy home and change her clothes. She shouldn't be out like this." But he, too, was *oblivious* to her words. It was as if Viola had become invisible!

The realization that no one could see or hear her was just beginning to sink in when Viola noticed her brother-in-law standing in the hall. He had just been approached by one of his neighbors and they struck up a conversation. The neighbor asked the in-law what he was doing at the hospital and also inquired about his plans for the upcoming weekend.

"Well, it looks like my sister-in-law is going to kick the bucket," he said. "I was planning to go to Athens, but I'll stick around now to be a pallbearer."

Viola was infuriated by this insensitive remark, but she had to face the fact that, for the moment, there wasn't much she could do about it. It seemed that she had attained a unique vantage point—one that many people only dream of—that of a fly on the wall!

Fortunately for Viola, she would have the opportunity to confront her brother-in-law about this little conversation sometime after her release from the hospital. Laughing, she would watch his face turn several shades of red while quoting him word for word. Though he would make quite an attempt to deny it, he eventually would give in, admitting that it was exactly what he had said.

But for now, Viola was trying to make some sense of the strange situation when she noticed that there were *presences* with her, whom she took to be angels. They didn't exactly look like angelic beings, at least not the way she had always envisioned, with wings, halos, and golden harps. Still, there was something about their presence that gave her a much needed sense of peace. She came to recognize them as her guardian angels and understood that they had always been with her.

Another exciting discovery was that she was able to travel anywhere her thoughts could take her. Instantly, after thinking that she would like to see her sister, Viola found herself in Rockville, Maryland, at her sister's home. She observed her sister getting ready to go to the grocery store. Viola took note of the clothes she was wearing, the search for misplaced keys and a lost grocery list, and finally, the car she drove to the store. Viola was feeling in no mood to go grocery shopping, so instead decided to visit another nearby sister. She was able to determine that this sister had also gone shopping. Like the conversation with her brother-in-law, all of these details would eventually be verified when Viola would have a chance to talk with her sisters.

While she puzzled over this peculiar disembodied condition, her guardian angels asked if she was ready to leave this area. Without any hesitation she replied, "Yes, I'm ready to go now."

All at once Viola felt herself being whisked in an upward motion through a long black tunnel. She had no idea how she entered the tunnel and noticed that the walls of the tunnel did not touch her. She was mesmerized by the radiant light at the end of the tunnel as it drew her ever closer. Faster and faster she went through this remarkable passageway. At one point she saw what she described as a "gray area" where she saw colorless souls shifting aimlessly about, apparently unable to transcend their earthly attachments. She did not linger there, but instead focused on the fantastic light up ahead.

Viola accelerated through the end of the tunnel, emerging into what appeared to her as a beautiful valley full of flowers, glistening rivers, and brilliant colors. Birds and animals dotted this magnificent landscape. Viola could think of no words to describe this place, for she had never seen anything like it. The world she had left behind was nothing but a pale imitation of this heavenly scene.

Everything was bathed in a glorious love and light. And somehow she understood that the light and the love were the same thing! This radiant loving light pulsated all around her and was so incredibly bright that she could not resist the temptation to look at it, yet it did not hurt her eyes. She felt that this love was alive and it was almost as if she could see it, touch it, and feel it.

Viola soon found that she was not alone in this wonderful place either. She encountered friends and family who had died before her. Although these people would initially appear to her at the age she had last seen them, she soon realized that they were all in the prime of life. They were filled with a great warmth and spoke to her, not in words, but in what can only be described as a kind of mental telepathy, in which there are no misunderstandings.

The first person she encountered was a childhood girlfriend who had died in the polio epidemic of the 1930s. Her friend was a loving woman who assured Viola that everything was fine and that she was happy. Viola's mother and her grandparents also came to greet her. She was overjoyed to see her mother and grandmothers again, and to meet her grandfathers for the first time, both of whom had died before she was born.

During this time a baby also appeared to her and said, "Hi, I'm your brother."

"I don't have a brother," Viola replied, somewhat baffled.

He then proceeded to show himself to her as a small infant dressed in a cap and a long dress with booties and socks. He told her, "Look me over now and remember how I looked this way and you can tell our father when you get back and he'll tell you what happened."

Later on in the hospital, after Viola would recover enough to talk, she would tell her father what she had seen and heard. He would shake his head in disbelief and reply, "Well I don't know how you knew that because nobody but your mother, the doctor, and I knew about these things." Viola discovered from her father that she did indeed have a brother who had died as an infant but had never been mentioned to the later children.

Viola was experiencing a joyous homecoming, overflowing with love. But the best was yet to come! It was at this time that she was approached by a warm, loving presence of extraordinary light that completely engulfed her. She felt that the light was an extremely masculine being, yet it also possessed what she considered to be softer, feminine qualities. Viola recognized this brilliant light—and later told me during our interview that she had known it to be Jesus. She reveled in His wonderful love which pulsated all around her. He totally accepted her and expressed forgiveness to her for everything she had ever done. But deep inside Viola wondered, could she ever forgive herself for some of her selfish ways?

And then she saw it—a panoramic view of her entire life. It unfolded before her in a dimension of time as she had never experienced. It seemed to be there *all at once!* It began with her birth and included every minute detail of her life right up to the present moment. There were no secrets, no hidden truths. She observed her earthly actions as though she were watching a movie while simultaneously having the sensation that she was actually living her entire life over again. Viola Horton became aware of every feeling, every thought, and every deed she had ever done and realized fully for the first time the implications of her actions on others.

As the events in Viola's life were reviewed, she was surprised to learn that it was not her outward success that received attention but rather the simple acts of kindness she had done. Many of her *big achievements*, which she had considered to be important, didn't count for very much here. She came to understand that it's the little things one does, like giving someone a helping hand, or hugging a child, anything done unselfishly, that matters most of all.

Viola was feeling a glorious peace wash over her soul. In this brilliant light she had found acceptance, forgiveness, and most of all, love—wonderful love. She never wanted to leave. And that is why she was absolutely devastated when she was asked by the light, "Are you ready to go back?"

"No, I want to go on to the city of light," she pleaded, glimpsing the amazing scenes that awaited her up ahead.

But again the voice came, "No. Don't you want to go back?"

She paused for a moment and listened. Someone was crying; it sounded like a young girl. Looking back over her shoulder, Viola was able to see her daughter and husband standing next to her hospital bed. They were trying desperately to hold on to the woman they both loved. She could hear her daughter's tearful pleas, "Mom don't go, come back to us. Mama, I need you. Mom, come back."

And then Viola was asked again, "Are you ready to go?"

She gazed off into the distance toward a city filled with splendid light. How she longed to go there, to stay in this wonderful place forever. But her daughter was counting on her; Viola couldn't let her down. So with a heavy heart she replied, "It seems that my daughter needs me . . . so I must go back."

"That is good, for it is not your time yet," came the voice.

And then it was over. As swiftly as Viola had left her body, she instantly returned. There was no tunnel, no beautiful light. Her spirit simply entered her body through the top of her head and she was immediately consumed by the pain and suffering of her earthly being.

The angels, who were still with her, told her that she would need to make some kind of sound or movement so that the doctors would know to keep fighting for her life. Viola found this request to be rather amusing since she had never felt more alive. She laughed out loud. The astonished doctors wasted no time in their efforts to restart her heart. Before leaving, the angels informed her that she would remain unconscious for three days in order to suppress some of the knowledge she had been given.

While Viola slept, her anxious family waited and prayed for her recovery. True to the angels' word, she awoke on the third day—a changed woman. It was several more days before she could speak and tell her family of her fantastic encounter.

She emerged from this experience with a great appreciation for people and most of all, the wonderful love that had been shown to her.

"Oh, I'm not perfect," she confesses. "I'm still human—I'm still selfish. But it has changed my way of thinking. It's made me a more understanding person of others. I think I'm a better person about watching out for the needs of others and not being always so selfish."

She answered many questions on that day of filming from those of us who wanted to know more about what she had learned from her time in the light. Viola said she was frequently asked about Hell. "Was it a fiery pit?" The answer she gave to us was quite straightforward and simple: "Well, what I found to be Hell was *separation from God. This* is a total Hell."

And leaving the presence of God's light that day was one of the most difficult things she ever had to face.

"I didn't want to return, and I would love to go back. Someday I will, and then hopefully I can stay and won't have to come back."

Although she spoke longingly of the day when she could return, she stressed that while here on Earth she felt a mission to love others the way she experienced while in the presence of God's loving light.

Over the next several years, my wife and I kept in touch with Viola and her husband, Jud, and they became like family. Upon hearing about the birth of our firstborn daughter, Viola sent us a beautiful baby quilt lovingly crafted by her grandmotherly hands.

Jud called us early in the spring of 1997 to tell us that Viola had finally returned to the Father. We all will miss her.

I couldn't help imagining that during her great homecoming, my own Dad may have been among those greeting her. I can almost hear him saying, "So, you're Viola! You don't know me, but I want to thank you . . ."

CHAPTER 18

Afterlife in the First Century

INCE MY INVOLVEMENT in the TV program *Life After Life*, I've gotten some stern warnings and objections from well-meaning and God-fearing religious people. Their message is typically that the popular interest in the near-death experience, and often in angels, is a cultish deception that is leading people down a dangerous road, and away from God.

As I myself have had a long and abiding faith in God, I have devoted quite a bit of reflection to trying to reconcile the accounts I have heard firsthand with what I have read in the Bible. I'm not a religious scholar, and if I'm wrong about the connections I make, God forgive me. But for what it's worth, here is why I think the current popularity in this subject is part of a divinely inspired wake-up call.

Many of the religious records that exist from the first century were written as personal, heartfelt letters to those whose love and trust were important. Luke was a physician and a good friend of Paul of Tarsus, who also wrote letters to friends around the Mediterranean, and those letters became a large part of what we know as the New Testament. In one of Paul's letters to the church in

Corinth he describes what seems by all accounts to be a near-death experience:

Although there is nothing to be gained, I will go on to visions and revelations from the Lord. I know a man in Christ who fourteen years ago was caught up to the third heaven. Whether it was in the body or out of the body I do not know—God only knows. And I know that this man—whether in the body or apart from the body I do not know, but God knows—was caught up to paradise. He heard inexpressible things, things that man is not permitted to tell.

Many Bible scholars believe that Paul was speaking of his own experience. If true, it makes the following excerpt from another of his letters even more intriguing, as he does an artful job of expressing "inexpressible things":

But someone may ask, "How are the dead raised?" How foolish! What you sow does not come to life unless it dies. When you sow, you do not plant the body that will be, but just a seed, perhaps of wheat or of something else. All flesh is not the same: Men have one kind of flesh, animals have another . . . There are also heavenly bodies and there are earthly bodies . . . So will it be with the resurrection of the dead. The body that is sown is perishable, it is raised imperishable; it is sown in weakness, it is raised in power; it is sown a natural body, it is raised a spiritual body . . . So it is written: "The first man Adam, became a living being," the last Adam a life-giving spirit . . . And just as we have borne the likeness of the earthly man, so shall we bear the likeness of the man from heaven.

I declare to you, brothers, that flesh and blood cannot inherit the kingdom of God, nor does the perishable inherit the imperishable. Listen, I tell you a mystery. We will not all sleep, but we will all be changed—in a flash, in the twinkling of an eye, at the last trumpet . . . For the perishable must clothe itself with the imperishable, and the mortal with immortality . . . then the saying that is written will come true:

"Death has been swallowed up in victory."
"Where, O death, is your victory?
"Where, O death, is your sting?"
    —1 CORINTHIANS 15:35–55

Death and resurrection, eternal life, paradise, and the Kingdom of Heaven are some of the major themes in the Gospels. I highlighted several of the key stories in the Bible about death, near-death, and the afterlife.

The New Testament contains three stories in which Jesus raised the dead back to life. In one account, his dear friend Lazarus had been dead and entombed four days before Jesus arrived. Jesus wept with the other mourners, and then shocked the family by asking to "take away the stone" that sealed off the tomb (and as someone there mentioned, sealed *in* the foul smell of death).

∾

"So they took away the stone. Then Jesus looked up and said, 'Father, I thank you that you have heard me. I knew that you always hear me, but I said this for the benefit of the people standing here, that they may believe that you sent me.'

"When he said this, Jesus called in a loud voice, 'Lazarus, come out!'" The dead man then hopped out, his hands and feet still mummified with strips of linen, and a cloth around his face.

Joyful at the sight of his old friend, but sympathetic to the comical scene before him, "Jesus said to them, 'Take off the grave clothes and let him go' (John 11:1–44)."

∾

Another story has Jesus arriving a bit too late to heal the dying daughter of Jairus, a ruler of the synagogue.

"Hearing this, Jesus said to Jairus, 'Don't be afraid; just believe, and she will be healed.'

"When he arrived at the house of Jairus, he did not let anyone go in with him except Peter, John, and James, and the child's father and mother. Meanwhile, all the people were wailing and mourning for her. 'Stop wailing,' Jesus said. 'She is not dead but asleep.'

"They laughed at him, knowing that she was dead. But he took her by the hand and said, 'My child, get up!' Her spirit returned, and at once she stood up. Then Jesus told them to give her something to eat. Her parents were astonished, but he ordered them not to tell anyone what had happened (Mark 5:21–43)."

∞

The last recorded episode of raising the dead describes Jesus approaching a funeral procession.

"As he approached the town gate, a dead person was being carried out— the only son of his mother, and she was a widow. And a large crowd from the town was with her.

"When the Lord saw her, his heart went out to her and he said, 'Don't cry.'

"Then he went up and touched the coffin, and those carrying it stood still. He said, 'Young man, I say to you, get up!'

"The dead man sat up and began to talk, and Jesus gave him back to his mother.

"They were all filled with awe and praised God. 'A great prophet has appeared among us,' they said. 'God has come to help his people.' This news about Jesus spread throughout Judea and the surrounding country (Luke 7:11–17)."

❧

Of course, these stories are not told from the same perspective as near-death experiences, which are usually from the point of view of the nearly deceased. They do, however, point to an authority that Jesus seemed to possess in the area of life and death. Christ's greatest legacy, and the climax of the Gospel story, was to rise from the grave himself after three days of entombment following his execution. And his death reportedly had a massive ripple effect on the entire realm of the afterlife.

"And when Jesus had cried out again in a loud voice, he gave up his spirit.

"At that moment the curtain of the temple was torn in two from top to bottom. The earth shook and the rocks split.

"The tombs broke open and the bodies of many holy people who had died were raised to life. They came out of the tombs, and after Jesus' resurrection they went into the holy city and appeared to many people (Matthew 27:50–53)."

According to tradition, the temple curtain had symbolized an impenetrable veil that existed between the people of Israel and the "holy of holy" place where God resided. Anyone who passed beyond the curtain would not survive. A torn curtain would signify a new passage, beyond death, directly into God's presence.

Some might ask, "Couldn't the so-called resurrection of Jesus have been just another case of a near-death experience?" It is unlikely. The Romans' well-practiced methods of flogging and crucifixion were designed to be both gruesome and terminal, bringing about maximum pain and ultimate death. It is highly improbable that he would have recovered naturally from his brutal flogging, crucifixion, and final spear stabbing, without some kind of supernatural intervention or power over death. We read, "There was a violent earthquake, for an angel of the Lord came down from heaven and, going to the tomb, rolled back the stone and sat on it. His appearance was like lightning, and his clothes were white as snow. The guards were so afraid of him that they shook and became like dead men (Matthew 28:2–4)."

I admit that prior to my investigations into contemporary supernatural phenomena, I might have taken the angelic descriptions with a grain of salt. But after hearing so many real people use similar terms—"brilliant being of light" or "bright as the sun," etc.—I am more inclined to accept the Gospel writer's report about the angel at face value.

All of the vivid imagery that is included in the accounts, whether taken literally or metaphorically, paints a scene of some momentous achievement by the death of Jesus.

I personally take the more literal interpretation for the following reason, and it ties directly to the stories I've heard from those who have come close to dying. When people undergo death, they often describe finding themselves in darkness. Only after they recognize a *light* off in the distance, which serves as a kind of beacon, do they know how to proceed into God's presence. Isn't that light—considering the qualities of compassion, forgiveness, and strength that are attributed to it (Him) in the NDE reports—the essence of Christ? Aside from all the religiosity that has been attached to Jesus over the centuries, it appears that Christ's greatest effect on humanity has been to light their darkness, in life and evidently also in death. There are many, many times in the Gospels where Christ is referred to in luminous terms, which are often taken poetically but which may also be seen as a literal description. And one finds countless references to light in the Old and New Testament:

"The Lord is my light and my salvation."   —PSALM 27:1

"After six days Jesus took with him Peter, James and John the brother of James, and led them up a high mountain by themselves. There he was transfigured before them. His face shone like the sun, and his clothes became as white as the light."
        —MATTHEW 17:1–2

"As [Saul] neared Damascus on his journey, suddenly a light from heaven flashed around him, 'Saul, Saul why do you persecute me?' 'Who are you, Lord?' Saul asked. 'I am Jesus, whom you are persecuting . . .'"   —ACTS 9:3–4

There are many other straightforward scriptural accounts of God depicted as a bright light. When allowed to be taken literally, and not passed off as poetic metaphor, one gets the sense that this Light is describing the very spark that we think of as life itself.

"Through him all things were made; without him nothing was made that has been made. In him was life, and that life was the light of men. The light shines in the darkness, but the darkness has not understood it."   —JOHN 1:3–5

Admittedly, there are some Christians who don't share my certainty about the identity of the Light whom we hear about in these experiences. The source of doubt is a Scripture in which St. Paul warns about false apostles:

For such men are false apostles, deceitful workmen, masquerading as apostles of Christ. And no wonder, for Satan himself masquerades as an angel of light.
    —2 CORINTHIANS 11:13–14

I find it hard to imagine that a dark spirit would sustain any impression of goodness and mercy to the degree that we consistently hear attributed to the Light in the near-death experience. Nevertheless, I personally believe in using discernment about spirits, and feel strongly about praying for direction in these areas.

To me, the identity of the Light is transparent. I am completely convinced that the Light whom people describe is the same presence whom I encountered as a young man when I asked Christ to reveal Himself to me. And the explosive love that filled my heart was just as hard to describe as the love that people say radiates from this Light.

Whatever one might personally believe about who Jesus was, it is revealing to know what He said about Himself:

> *"I am the light of the world. Whoever follows me will never walk in darkness, but will have the light of life."* —JOHN 8:12

And in the context of death and the afterlife, particularly in respect to all the reports about the Light from contemporary near-death experiences, it is also significant that Luke would say:

> *"... the Christ would suffer and, as the first to rise from the dead, would proclaim light to his own people and to the Gentiles."* —ACTS 26:23

If I can speculate, I would say that the big news of the first century was that a major obstacle was overcome in regard to human spiritual events, specifically in the area of death and the afterlife.

PART FOUR

Millennial Reflections

Beyond Time

STRANGE THING HAPPENED shortly after completing the film version of *Life After Life*. We sent a video copy to John Egle, who had been editor at Mockingbird, the original publisher of Raymond Moody's book *Life After Life*. John had been helpful to us in arranging the television rights for the title and other details, so I was eager to hear his reaction to the finished film.

Mr. Egle phoned after reviewing the tape and was very complimentary about our treatment of the subject, and its sensitivity toward the testimonial interviews. Feeling honored and grateful for his appreciation, I was then surprised by his next comment.

John said, "I have a question, though, about the editing of your interviews."

Oh, I thought to myself, *I wonder what's coming.*

"I'm wondering if there was anything in particular that you *didn't* include in the film. You know, outtakes on the cutting room floor?"

"Well, actually, yes." My mind zipped through the twenty hours of footage we had whittled down into a one-hour program. "There were quite a few elements in the various interviews that, for one reason or another, didn't make it into our film."

John laughed, like a traveler recalling a familiar journey. "Let me tell you what happened fifteen years ago.

"When Dr. Moody brought me his original manuscript, my wife and I read it through several times, utterly amazed. Remember, that was in the early seventies and we had never heard of anything like it before.

"There was a point in the manuscript that we felt sounded just too strange for the average reader to grasp. And we were concerned that this ground-breaking research of Moody's would be shrugged off and not taken seriously.

"So we made an editorial decision. We divided the manuscript into two stacks. The first section, about two thirds of the manuscript, was released as *Life After Life*. The last one third we held for nearly two years, during which time Moody refined it. It was then released as *Reflections on Life After Life*."

John added that many readers are still more familiar with the earlier elements of the near-death experience—the out-of-body state, the tunnel, the light, the life review, etc.—than they are with the further elements.

He said, "You ended your film at exactly the same point that we did the book."

He was right, and although I really wanted to include some of the more far-reaching material, it just didn't work for various reasons. One interview developed audio problems. With another, the film stock ran out. In a third, the guest got tired and her energy level sagged. Try as we might, we just couldn't build a strong ending with those later stages of people's experiences.

FURTHER JOURNEYS

Many of the additional aspects of the NDE have since been presented in other books released in the 1990s. Several gained popularity, and some met with controversy and resistance, just as Egle had predicted. Betty Eadie's

Embraced by the Light was joined by Dannion Brinkley's *Saved by the Light*, Sandra Roger's *Lessons from the Light*, and several other "— — — *by the Light"* titles. Each described a little bit more of the outlying regions of Heaven. Each author wrote about one or more of the elements that had not been presented previously. Still, there were some things that even those authors would not speak of. This, to me, was a vivid example of how popular thought (or what some call "collective awareness") must grow at its own natural pace; new ideas can only be built upon a general consensus of already accepted ideas.

I want to push open some squeaky doors because I feel the time is right to do so. To some readers, these will not be new ideas. In fact, most people will recognize familiar but perhaps forgotten concepts. When I heard some of the following experiences, they evoked memories of ancient writings, and they also touched something deep within my heart.

Some people report that during their close call with death, they arrive in a lovely pastoral setting, beautiful beyond words. The flowers are vibrant with colors that cannot be described. The plants, trees, birds, and animal life radiate light from within. This light seems to be the life source for all living things, and some people sense an exquisite feeling of *love* being emitted from these surroundings. The overall effect gives the deceased a euphoric feeling of well-being—of being in Paradise.

There is sometimes a barrier that seems to keep the person from progressing farther—often a river. The understanding is that once the barrier is crossed, there is usually no going back. Beyond the barrier, some speak of seeing a great city of light, with residences, centers of learning, libraries, and other structures populated by souls who are joyfully engaging in all kinds of activities. In one story I heard, a woman described a closer glimpse—the elaborately detailed interiors of huge homes she was enabled to visit—before she had to return to her body. Again, even the materials of the architecture are nearly always described as being composed of "pure light," imparting a beautiful glow to the entire landscape.

But not all experiences are as idyllic as the scenes described above. Although such stories are rare, several NDEs have reported a hellish realm. Some speak of a burning fire with demonic tormentors, and others describe a total blackness devoid of the love of God. One man says he found himself in the presence of pure evil. Ian McCormick underwent a dramatic NDE after repeated stings from a lethal box jellyfish while diving off the coast of Australia. While his body was convulsing, he recalled his mother once telling him, "Son, no matter how far from God you are, if you will but call out to Him from your heart, God will hear you." He uttered what he could remember of the Lord's Prayer: "Forgive us our sins . . ." Then, slipping away into a desolate and evil darkness, he asked himself, *Where am I?* Immediately a malevolent voice hissed at him, "Shut up! You are in Hell . . . You *deserve* to be here!" Confused and afraid, Ian replied, "But . . . I prayed to God . . ." At that instant, a radiant shaft of pure white light pierced the darkness above him and he was drawn into it. It is hard to say why we hear so few of these negative elements from NDE reports. Maybe those who undergo a trip to a hellish realm are less inclined to admit it, or perhaps it is blocked from their memory.

We discussed in earlier chapters the reports of a *gray area*, where souls wander aimlessly in denial of the loving light of God, which is evidently right there, but which they choose to ignore. It is worth repeating here that it seems to be a willful choice that individuals make between remaining in this closed off state, or moving on into the light. But the tendency seems to be for those who have chosen (in the same way they may have chosen their conditions during life) to remain there after death. Some theologians argue that this suggests a risky notion of postponing the decision to live a godly life, opting for a second chance to pursue wordly ambitions. It seems to me, though, a matter of recognizing that *eternity is here and now,* and that willful decisions we make in life provide momentum for the afterlife. Why wait to die to be in God's light if we can benefit from His influence while still alive?

Discarding the idea that eternity—whether Heaven or Hell—only exists in the afterlife, George Ritchie explains, "I have learned that life is eternal. Death is nothing more or less than a doorway, something you walk through." And another near-death survivor, Dr. George Rodonaia, puts it poetically. "I saw life as an infinite light, as an everlasting being. We cannot die because we are already created to live forever. The dimension of spirit is everlasting life. Death does not exist. We just pass through, like a railway station, going from one place to another."

Precognition

A Gallup poll revealed that approximately eight million Americans have had some kind of near-death experience. That is nearly one out of twenty persons. A further poll determined the percentages among them that had experienced each of the commonly reported elements. One third of all NDEs reported a life review. One out of six encountered the Light. Only a tenth had a tunnel experience. *And the least common element, averaging about six percent of those surveyed, was the experience of precognition.*

Precognition is the phenomenon of seeing the future. Some report only seeing quick glimpses or flashes of events, while others can describe what they saw in greater detail. These visions may be personal in scope, or may encompass global events far into the future. Several predictions of upcoming events have been documented by researchers, and then later have come to pass. Dannion Brinkley, who went on record with Dr. Moody, accurately foretold several events including the precise date and location of the Gulf War.

Another aftereffect of the NDE that some people seem to develop is what might be best described as extrasensory perception. I have witnessed this ability and believe it is authentic. One speculation I have heard is that people become sensitized to divine or angelic messages following their passage through the spiritual veil. The suggestion is that divine messages are frequently sent but rarely received under normal circumstances. I understand that most recipients of these gifts downplay their abilities, not wanting to draw attention from the more profound messages they receive about the importance of loving others.

In particular, there is one aspect of precognition in the NDE that is still shrouded in mystery. In fact, most who have experienced this specific kind of glimpse into the future are almost secretive about it, as if bound by a code of silence. This involves the witnessing of *global visions*, encompassing major events in the world's future. Rather than going into prophetic details, let me explain why I think people are reluctant to discuss it.

Often, the visions they see are not clearly explained to them. So, as one woman explained it to me, "When I saw an earthquake, for example, the devastation was up-close and all encompassing. But just like when you see a close-up of a riot on TV news, it can look bigger than life. So it was with these visions of calamities. There were no reference points to indicate if these were just terrible disasters or the end of the world." Therefore—and I heard this reasoning time and again—those who see future visions don't want to frighten others unnecessarily by suggesting end-of-the-world scenarios. "People tend to react in fear and panic whenever they think something bad will happen. And the odds of something actually happening increase dramatically when many people anticipate that event. Like the stockmarket crash of 1929, they can create the very thing they fear."

So why are people permitted to witness future events if they are then discouraged from talking about them? The answer I have gleaned from some of these reluctant visionaries is through their sense of urgency to spread what they consider to be truly important messages. Two key terms come up frequently when asked about the root purpose of their view beyond time: *love* and *free will.*

LOVE

The most consistent messages people bring back from their otherworldly journeys is the dire need for humanity to learn how to love. Consider the answers from various near-death survivors when asked, *"What is the most important lesson you learned?"*:

1. *How to love other people . . . How to forgive and put yourself in the place of other people, in order to understand them . . . in order to love people . . . in order to love yourself. If you hold grudges, it hurts you and it hurts the other people. It's a barrier to love if you can't forgive. You don't necessarily have to forget when people hurt you, but you have to understand them and forgive them. I think that is the most important thing I found . . . looking at how we are* alike *rather than how we are different.*

2. *This is the main message I brought back, that love cannot be changed. This is everlasting, and love is always together with life. Love is what keeps this world alive. Love is in eternity. Love is a basic of humankind, and we are alive because of love.*

3. *The NDE had a lot of effects in changing my life. It's made me a more understanding person of others. I'm still selfish. I'm still a human. But it has changed my way of thinking.*

4. *And if people could understand that if they would pay more attention to each other, to care for and have faith and hope in each other, we could also begin to believe and have faith and hope in the true nature of the love of God. And not God in a religious value but God in a spiritual value. That through love all things are truly possible.*

FREE WILL

Frequently, these people get the understanding that the future is *not* carved in stone, and that their glimpses are *possibilities* or even *probabilities* of what could happen *if* humanity makes certain choices. The operative principle is *free will*.

During Dr. George Ritchie's extended tour of the heavenly realms, he was shown an amazing panoramic vision of the future. "The Christ extended His arm, and there before me opened up something like a corridor. And down that corridor I could see a series of events happening in the world, like a chain reaction. Every choice that people made had consequences attached that led to other events. And I saw man-made disasters and horrible things that humanity brought upon themselves. Things got worse and worse, with wars and terrible catastrophes. Finally I saw it culminating in the worst explosion you can ever imagine . . . And remember, my experience happened in the early days of WWII, before Hiroshima and Nagasaki. But this was far worse than that, and I knew it meant an end to life as we know it.

"And then," George went on to say, "that corridor closed up. He stretched out his hand again, and I saw another corridor opening. And I realized this was an alternate scenario—what might happen if humanity took another course. In this panorama, I could see people making choices and decisions based on love for others. And the consequences of the decisions of individuals made a different chain of events. People and nations began to get along, and I could see the world truly entering into a new millennium."

That was the last stage of Dr. Ritchie's near-death experience, after which he was immediately ushered back to his body, where he was revived to live again. And as I mentioned in an earlier chapter, George Ritchie's NDE was the one of the first in a long series of investigations, inspiring worldwide research into near-death studies and all the subsequent inquiries into spiritual matters.

When I had the chance to ask this pivotal character what he considered to be the most crucial insight for humanity, he answered:

"This is the most important thing that I have learned. When God gave us free will, *He also gave us the responsibility of suffering the consequences of using that free will . . . if we do not use it under His guidance.*"

People seem to have struggled with that *blessing/curse* since human history began. But if we have the choice of separating from God and going our own way, then we also have the choice of inviting Him to guide us by surrendering our will to His. Eventually, the desires of our heart reflect His desires, and vice versa. Many individuals from diverse backgrounds have learned to submit their strong will to the guidance of God's Spirit, and have found themselves stronger for it. *"The meek shall inherit the Earth . . ."* and *"One must give up one's life to find it . . ."* It may be life's greatest irony.

Enlarging that scenario to a global scale, in which individuals develop a one-on-one intimacy with God, one heart at a time, the love that results can have a dramatic effect on humanity's future history. The direction of the world is made by the collective choices of individuals, whether they choose to be self-serving or to serve others. Individuals can devote their lives to doing God's will and, as Jesus embodied (and some like St. Francis of Assisi emulated), do it regardless of the trappings of institutionalized religion. If humanity could agree with Christ's prayer to the Father, "May Your Kingdom come, Your will be done, on Earth as it is in Heaven," then the answer could connect us all to a power beyond ourselves, and beyond human imagination.

CHAPTER 20

Spreading the Word

AUL ROBERT WALKER is a historian and writer, and one of the authors I interviewed for *Stories of Miracles*. We hit it off immediately when he came to Nashville, and I enjoyed his perspective as a thinker plus his talent as a writer. We chatted for hours about miracles, history, science, and computers. Among Paul's books (which include a wonderful coffee table edition for National Geographic called *Trail of the Wild West*), is a paperback collection of uplifting stories entitled *Every Day's a Miracle*. In it he presents some fascinating historical miracles, which became the focus of our television interview.

Paul is an up-to-date, twenty-first-century researcher who uses the Internet to find facts and documents for his books, and also to connect with some interesting modern-day stories while on-line. He shared some of his research techniques with me and we conducted an experiment while on-line and on-camera. With videotape rolling, Paul did an impromptu Web search for stories of angels, miracles, and near-death experiences. I immediately got the picture that these encounters are no longer just the subject of books, magazines, and television shows. People daily are posting their own real-life stories in countless bulletin boards the world over, and although the accounts aren't always easy to verify, the sheer volume of stories is impressive.

Here are just a couple of the postings we found:

SUBJECT: *Re: In Search of Angels*
DATE: 03-15 20:09:12 *EDT*
FROM: *Scottie*
TO: *JS (posted in response to another posting)*

I have also had an experience with an angel, and I believe firmly that it is the only explanation to this story of mine.

One night I was coming home from work, driving on the interstate. It was July 4th and approximately 11:45 P.M.. I was just about the only car on the interstate at that time. I was getting ready to get on the exit ramp, when my steering wheel sharply turned to the left, putting me in the fast lane of the interstate. Seconds later, a car came speeding the wrong way down the exit ramp I was about to enter. If I had exited on that ramp, my passenger and I would surely have been killed in a head-on accident. There was no sign of that car when I was about to exit, but surely my angel must have seen what was about to happen. I'm sure it was an angel that turned my wheel sharply, as I didn't know why this was happening. Please tell me your experience.

And another posting reads:

SUBJECT: *Angels*
DATE: 04-10 21:43:30 *EDT*
FROM: *TA*

I don't know so much if this was an angel. At the time I surely believed that Jesus Himself had touched me. You see, my mother was dying of cancer. She was the only family I had left. The loss of my mother was devastating to me, she was truly my best friend. One night I was crying uncontrollably in bed when I felt a hand press ever so softly on my back, and my entire body became warm. When I turned around to see who it was, there was no one there. I stopped crying and the warmth continued to fill my body. I truly believe that it was Jesus who touched me that night. Although my mother still died, I felt like Jesus was telling me things would be O.K. He would always be there for me.

And the third of many Internet postings we found echoed a conversation that Paul and I had just finished:

SUBJECT: QUANTUM PHYSICS & RELIGION
DATE: 05-07 11:59:55 EDT
FROM: RIOTECHS

The old Newtonian physics did away with God by its mechanistic outlook on the universe. Quantum physics has returned God to us. Mystics through the ages have always known there is a higher power that was an intrinsic part of everything that exists within ourselves, the world, the entire universe. They knew that God or the light existed within. Quantum physicists are now agreeing with this very same outlook. They are now saying that all matter is energy and that on the subatomic level this same energy exists in everything. They do not understand it and cannot describe it, only that it exists. But they recognize that it is this energy that is the cause of all existence. Sounds like "God" to me. Please respond.

Like signposts for the coming millennium, we are witnessing a new technical capability to share stories, beliefs, and theories with others via the Internet. This decentralization of information will soon allow virtually anyone to publish their writings, and even broadcast audio and video to the world. And the expanded ability to share real-life experiences and insights will further expand our collective learning. The impact on society will be remarkable and will add a whole new chapter to the story of humanity's quest for truth and meaning.

I read a wonderful book called *A Short History of the World,* by H. G. Wells. The visionary author of futuristic fiction was also a renowned historian. His quick-stroke illustrations of the milestones in world history are illuminating, and show a clear picture of civilization's turning points. In his chapter on the *"Priests and Prophets of Judea,"* Wells describes how, against all odds, the relatively small Jewish culture became an enduring society based upon two unique features.

One of Judaism's distinctions was its radical view that "God was invisible and remote, an invisible God in a temple not made with hands, a Lord of Righteousness throughout the earth. All other peoples had national gods embodied in images that lived in temples. If the image was smashed and the temple razed, presently that god died out."

Judaism's second historical milepost, linked to its worship of one God, was the introduction of a written, and thus portable, collection of stories. These records were reminders to future generations of the miraculous dealings between God and His people. The Jews survived captivity in Babylon and many other hardships. "And they were able to do this," wrote Wells, "because they had gotten together this literature of theirs, their Bible . . . It is not so much the Jews who made the Bible, as the Bible which made the Jews. Jerusalem was from the first only their nominal capital; their real city was this book of books. This is a new sort of thing in history. It is something of which the seeds were sown long before, when the Sumerians and Egyptians began to turn their hieroglyphics into writing. The Jews were a new thing, a people often without a king and presently without a temple (for as we shall tell

Jerusalem itself was broken up in A.D. 70), held together and consolidated out of heterogeneous elements by nothing but the power of the written word."[5]

So the development of the *written word* of the Jewish Bible stripped the ancient pagan priests of their centralized control over religion. It gave unity to the religious ideas of geographically scattered people. Johannes Gutenberg's invention of moveable type in the mid 1400s had a similar effect of deregulating religion when the Bible became the first work ever published, taking it out of the exclusive domain of the priesthood and putting it in the hands of the masses. The trend always moves away from a priestly middleman and toward a personal relationship with God. Freedom of religion allows people to pray to God intimately, one to one. Freedom of expression encourages people to think for themselves, and to freely share their collected thoughts and experiences. And this democracy of ideas is exactly what our present technology is allowing, instantly and globally.

All along the path of humanity's quest for the Kingdom of Heaven, *written signposts* have helped steer individuals closer to a direct and personal relationship with God in the temple of their own hearts.

"The time is coming" declares the Lord, "when I will make a new covenant with the house of Israel and with the house of Judah.

"I will put my law in their minds, and write it on their hearts. I will be their God, and they will be my people.

"No longer will a man teach his neighbor, or a man his brother, saying, 'Know the Lord,' because they will all know me, from the least of them to the greatest," declares the Lord.

5. Wells, H. G. *A Short History of the World.* New York: Macmillan, 1922), pp. 123–24.

"For I will forgive their wickedness and will remember their sins no more."

—JEREMIAH 31:31, 33–34 (600 B.C.)

CHAPTER 21

The First Coming

Once, having been asked by the Pharisees when the kingdom of God would come,
Jesus replied, "The kingdom of God does not come with your careful observations,
nor will people say, 'Here it is,' or 'There it is,' because the kingdom of God is
within you."

—LUKE 17:20–21

 HAVE ALWAYS HAD DIFFICULTY balancing the notions of the vengeful, judgmental God of the Old Testament with the compassionate and loving Father figure that Jesus preached about. Then I
became a father myself and realized that in order to be loving, I
have to be both firm and compassionate. And as my children grow and learn,
I can spend less time disciplining and more time communicating. In simple
terms, this seems to be the progress that God has made with his children.

The Old Covenant, which was a mutual vow or contract, proposed that *if*
God's people followed His laws, *then* they would inherit His Kingdom. But
His people were rebellious. God spelled out consequences for misbehavior,
and then allowed His children to suffer the results of bad choices. As straightforward as the agreement sounded, people were typically self-absorbed and
broke the contract, again and again.

Still, it seems that God loved His people enough to make a *New Covenant.* Through the Prophet Isaiah, in around 700 B.C., God promised to send a Messiah: "Here is my servant, whom I uphold, my chosen one in whom I delight; I will put my Spirit on him and he will bring justice to the nations." And in the prophecy, God blessed the Messiah: "I the Lord, have called you in righteousness; I will take hold of your hand. I will keep you and will *make you to be a covenant for the people,* and a *light* for the Gentiles, to open eyes that are blind, to free captives from prison and to release from the dungeon those who sit in *darkness* (Isaiah 42:1–7)."

Were these ancient prophecies—in which God promised a guiding light to draw souls out of darkness—offering the very light described by George Ritchie, Viola Horton, and many others who have crossed over into death?

The prophet Daniel wrote, "In my vision at night I looked, and there before me was one like a *son of man,* coming with the clouds of heaven. He approached the Ancient of Days and was led into his presence. He was given authority, glory and sovereign power; all peoples, nations and men of every language worshiped him. His dominion is an everlasting dominion that will not pass away, and his kingdom is one that will never be destroyed." In essence, the prophet was saying there would be a great Day of Judgment. The Messiah would lead God's people in a triumphant battle against their oppressor, and those on the side of light would share the victory, and the darkness would be extinguished. He would reclaim the kingdom for God's people and would reign as their king forever (Daniel 7:13–14).

Again, this age-old messianic prophecy seems to be describing what I have heard so often from those who have glimpsed eternity. Consider the dynamics of the visionary scenes: an extraordinarily bright and powerful being to whom all souls are drawn; His firm but compassionate judgment while reviewing each individual's life; His total forgiveness for all sins or selfish misdeeds; and His opening of the door to an eternal, everlasting kingdom, city, or paradise—effectively defeating death.

Isaiah and the other prophets of Israel went on to describe—in great detail through extraordinary visions of fantastic symbolism—the process by which the kingdom would come. These visionary accounts have become known as *apocalyptic* prophecies, and efforts to decipher them have played an influential role in world history. But there are no simple interpretations to the prophecies, which tend to be surrealistic in their imagery and abstract in their plots. Throughout history, attempts to interpret them in terms of current events have fallen flat and typically with disastrous side effects.

Civilization has been forcefully directed by the understandings, and *misunderstandings*, of these powerful concepts, alternately called apocalyptic, millennial, or end time prophecies. Actually, there is a difference between *apocalypticism* and *millenarianism* (mil-le-NAR-i-an-ism). Now is a fitting time to take a closer look at these and other prophecies—at our particular moment in history, this epic crossroad entering the third millennium.

THE ROOTS OF MISCONCEPTION

In the scholarly field of eschatology, which deals with the concept of the end of time, *apocalyptic* prophesies can be found in many religions and have similar themes. Generally, they paint a scenario in which mankind has failed to support God's plan and through a series of events the world comes to a fiery end. This ending usually signals a new beginning, which is sometimes described as a restoration of the original paradise from which humanity fell.

The Jewish prophets were not unique in their visions. Zoroaster was a Persian priest turned prophet whose visions established a religious system in which Ormazd was worshiped, god of creation, light, and goodness. The prophecies spoke of an age-old struggle between the god of light and the evil spirit of darkness, and a future transformation that would end the conflict forever. Following a worldwide resurrection of the dead, a final judgment would destroy the wicked and immortalize the righteous. Interestingly, the modern-day Islamic word *jihad*, or holy war, has its roots in a similar concept of a supernatural war in heaven between the powers of light and darkness.

For many Jews who heard the prophecies of Isaiah, Daniel, Ezekiel, and others, the new ideas of a bodily resurrection and an eternal kingdom were tremendous and brought great hope. Before that time, there had been no prospect beyond the grave for those who died and went to that shadowy place called Sheol. But the prophecies were revolutionary in other ways, too, and caused stressful shifts in the paradigms of social and religious thinking. The old concept of God's Chosen People as exclusive heirs to the Kingdom had changed. The righteous ones could now include the Gentiles. God's Kingdom was no longer limited to a geographic area. The great battle between light and dark was no longer just fought between men of various nations, but in Heaven, between the angelic forces of God and the rebellious legions of the enemy. In short, these messianic and apocalyptic prophesies had changed the old rules, and those who were accustomed to thinking in terms of the Chosen People and the Gentiles, us and them, good guys versus bad guys, had to face a big adjustment. The conflicting interpretations of these cryptic visions sowed seeds of misunderstandings that grew into thickly entwined, and often contradictory, expectations among the Jews.

By the time Jesus appeared on the scene, several Jewish factions shouted slogans with apocalyptic messages. The Essenes were a deeply spiritual sect, and were eagerly awaiting the Messiah. John the Baptist, who announced, "Repent, for the Kingdom of Heaven is near," is believed to have ranked among them. The Essenes were studying Scriptures and storing scrolled copies in jars near the Dead Sea, deep in a cave—just in case. They were preparing for the final battle between the "Sons of Light and the Sons of Darkness"—training celibate monks in Qumran to fight against those forces—in whatever form they might appear. The Zealots were another sect that prophesied the coming time of salvation and were expecting the Messiah to rise up as a military leader. They refused allegiance to the pagan emperor and called for an overthrow of Roman domination. These Zealots tried to actively trigger the revolution with calculated uprisings. The Pharisees, Sadducees, and the Sanhedrin council were the official Jewish religious leaders. Although they argued among themselves about doctrinal issues, they were politically in the pocket of Rome, and worked hard at opposing the rebellious factions.

When Jesus arrived, He was heralded by many as the Messiah, and eventually acknowledged it Himself. "Again the high priest asked him, 'Are you the Christ [Messiah], the Son of the Blessed One?' Jesus said, 'I am. And you will see the Son of Man sitting at the right hand of the Mighty One and coming on the clouds of heaven (Mark 14:61–62).'" But he had to fight the tides of popular expectation regarding exactly what the Messiah was and what the fight for God's Kingdom was all about. Once, having been asked by the Pharisees when the Kingdom of God would come, Jesus replied, "The Kingdom of God does not come with your careful observations, nor will people say, 'Here it is,' or 'There it is,' *because the kingdom of God is within you* (Luke 17:20–21)." He spent the majority of His ministry trying to correct people's thinking about the true nature of the Kingdom of God, for which we find over a hundred references in the Gospels. "Jesus, knowing that they intended to make him king by force, withdrew again to a mountain by himself." Even at the very end, when King Herod's guards came to arrest Him,

Jesus tried to explain, "Am I leading a rebellion, that you have to come out with swords and clubs to capture me? (Matthew 26:55)." Brought before the Sanhedrin, He was tried on revolutionary charges: "Then some stood up and gave this false testimony against him, 'We heard him say: *I will destroy this man-made temple and in three days will build another, not made by man*' (Mark 14:57–58)." Ultimately facing the Roman governor Pontius Pilate, Jesus was asked about His Kingdom. "Jesus said, 'My kingdom is not of this world. If it were, my servants would fight to prevent my arrest by the Jews . . . my kingdom is from another place' (John 18:36)."

If, as Jesus said, the Messiah's Kingdom was in Heaven, then was the battleground also in a spiritual, nonmaterial realm? And if the enemy was not Rome or any political foe, but instead some underlying forces of darkness, then wouldn't the misunderstanding among those who anticipated a worldly battle be catastrophic? History books reveal that a catastrophe is *exactly* what resulted.

In A.D. 66 the fanatical Zealot party brought about their eagerly awaited revolution. The Roman garrison was overrun, and Jerusalem fell into the rebels' hands, but only temporarily. Rome responded with an army of eighty thousand men, using their well-rehearsed siege tactics. In A.D. 70 Jerusalem was reduced to rubble by the Romans, and the Great Temple was burned and toppled. The historian Josephus was an eyewitness to the terrible sufferings of the besieged city, detailed in his *History of the Wars of the Jews*. Five hundred Jewish rebels a day were crucified, until there were no more trees but a forest of crosses. The Sadducees and the Sanhedrin were extinguished forever. In the end, the Jews who had not been massacred were sold into slavery. The nation of Israel was finished, and would leave scarcely a trace in history for nearly two thousand years.

Was this what the prophets of Israel had predicted? As climactic as the battle was, it hadn't gone as many had expected. Where was the promised Kingdom of God? And where was the king? If the enemy had been defeated, then why were the Romans still in charge? Disappointment wrung heavily in disillusioned hearts of countless numbers.

Yet for many others the Gospel story continued to unfold and the messianic prophecies took on a new dimension—a fully spiritual one. The prayer of Jesus to the Father, "Your kingdom come, your will be done, on Earth as it is in Heaven," became one of the primary strategic weapons against the enemy. And the new battle cry was the call to *love one another."* In this way the final battle would be won—one heart at a time.

But the message wasn't clear to everyone that the war was not waged outwardly but inwardly, not politically but personally, because in the two millennia that followed, the historic misunderstanding of the prophecies would resurface like a recurring bad dream.

What Is the Millennium?

Most contemporary people understand that the word "millennium" refers to a thousand-year span of time. But many don't realize that the term "millennium" as it relates to end times comes from the prophetic Book of Revelation, chapter twenty. It was written in the first century by a man named John, who was fully convinced that the Christian faith would overcome the demonic forces in the world in the very near future. John's mysterious vision resembles the imagery of the earlier apocalyptic prophets. In it an angel, holding a key in one hand and a chain in the other, comes out of Heaven and casts Satan into the Abyss for a millennium—a thousand years. During that time, those who had been martyred on Christ's behalf would be resurrected. "They came to life and reigned with Christ for a thousand years." This is the *millennium.* "When the thousand years is over, Satan will be released from his prison and will go out to deceive the nations in the four corners of the earth—Gog and Magog—to gather them for battle."

The prophetic *millennium* is not a reference to the calendar; not the year A.D. 1000., A.D. 2000., nor any other millennium date. It refers to a *time span* within a supernatural scenario. Trying to logically link it to our natural time-space vantage point would be futile, although many have tried. There is much more to the prophetic imagery of Revelation, and endless debates have raged attempting to tie its symbolic events with current events from nearly every generation from the first century to now.

Significantly, the battle imagery is projected once again by Revelation and readers are challenged to decide if this war is to be waged with physical or spiritual weapons. This should be a question of major importance, for as civilization progresses, so does its weaponry. A misinterpretation, or a deceptive interpretation, could have increasingly ominous consequences. Many different spins have been given to the reading of Revelation, and the variables are multiplied when trying to align them with assorted Old Testament prophecies, and with the predictions made by Jesus.

What Did Jesus Say?

Of all the end times prophecies, those foretold by Christ Himself are the most clear and least ambiguous. "Jesus left the Great Temple and was walking away when his disciples came to him to call his attention to its buildings. 'Do you see all these things?' he asked. 'I tell you the truth, not one stone here will be left on another; every one will be thrown down.' As Jesus was sitting on the Mount of Olives, the disciples came to him privately. 'Tell us,' they said, 'when will this happen, and what will be the sign of you coming and of the end of the age?'"

Jesus then described many specific natural disasters, and some general circumstances that would preface the end: Earthquakes. Famines. Persecutions. Wars and rumors of wars. Although most of these things do occur at any time in history, no matter how one interprets His words it seems obvious that He expected an ending of some kind, that the world as people know it would end. But He also made it very clear that "No one knows about that last day or hour, not even the angels in heaven, nor the Son, but only the Father." In fact, He warned against spending time pursuing predictions of His return in the clouds: "The time is coming when you will long to see one of the days of the Son of Man, but you will not see it. Men will tell you, 'There he is!' or 'Here he is!' Do not go running off after them." His bottom-line advice to his followers was simply to be ready. In a parable, He told His disciples, "Be on guard! Be alert! You do not know when that time will come. It's like a man going away: He leaves his house and puts his servants in charge, each with his assigned task, and tells the one at the door to keep watch. Therefore keep watch because you do not know when the owner of the house will come back—whether in the evening, or at midnight, or when the rooster crows, or at dawn. If he comes suddenly, do not let him find you sleeping . . ."

Some scholars suggest that portions of Jesus' prophecies addressed the end of the society—and the individuals—He was speaking to, citing several events that soon did come to pass, like the destruction of the Temple, and of Jerusalem itself. In hindsight, even though His disciples did not witness the end of the world, Jesus gave universally sound advice. On a personal level, each individual's "end of time" can happen without warning. In the past two millennia, societies and civilizations have seen many ends, often cataclysmic.

But being ready for disaster is different from courting it. *Millenarianism* is the name scholars have given to the belief—which has gripped the imagination of segments of society from time to time—that their own generation is the final one. And far too often, as we shall see in several stories, individuals have been manipulated by *faith mixed with fear,* into a frantic expectation. The story becomes tragic when that wishfulness becomes manifest, as with the religious Zealots, into attempts to *bring about the end.*

It's the End of the World
. . . Again

Generations come and generations go,
but the earth remains forever.
Whatever is has already been,
and what will be has been before;
and God will call the past to account.
—ECCLESIASTES 1:4 & 3:15

T MAY SEEM ODD to include a section on the *end of the world* and *doomsday cults* in a book called *Reflections of Heaven*. But when spirituality and religion meet a millennial milestone, then the subject of end times comes up naturally, and can't be ignored. Whether we realize it or not, we are being influenced, directly and indirectly, by contemporary scenarios that have roots over twenty-five centuries old.

We have already been hearing—and will continue to hear, long after the millennial fireworks celebrations have echoed away—apprehensive predictions of the end of the world. Technological disasters. Earth changes. Economic collapse. Sightings of Mary. Armageddon. White buffaloes.

Antichrists. Hopi prophecy. News about Israel. These "signs of the time," as they are often called, have shown up in every wavelength of the spiritual spectrum. The millennial rollover into the twenty-first century follows a long tradition of millennialist thinking, and the world-shaking expectations that go along with it.

As we have seen, people throughout recorded history have eagerly antici-pated the end of suffering, persecution, and the evils of the world. Prophets the world over have supported the beliefs that the end of the age of darkness is near. It is a perfectly natural and normal phenomenon, and might be con-sidered a vital stage in humanity's collective soul-searching—part of people's quest for *God's Kingdom*.

History shows a surprisingly long legacy of millenarian episodes, because dates ending with "000" are just one way of defining the millennium. With all the millennial crossroads in the past, the notion that *the end is near* is often signaled by the warnings by particular groups of vocal believers. And those warnings are often backed up by certain patterns of preparation, changes of lifestyle, and shifts in attitude. It is the actions of *some* of those zealous believ-ers, particularly those on the fringes of popular beliefs, that need to be watched.

My intention is neither to alarm anyone nor to dismiss the importance of being prepared; as Christ said, to *keep watch*. I believe with all my heart that the battle between light and darkness is very real, and is perhaps the core challenge and purpose for our lives. But I also think it is a matter of ultimate importance, especially at the major milestone of the third millennium, to monitor the mental climate of apocalyptic thinking. Often, in times past, the heat generated by those sincerely convinced of the imminent final conflict has ignited fires of confrontation. Suspicions, fears, and disappointments have historically conjured up the inner demons of racism, nationalism, and the worst kind of religious contention, namely the *holy war*. It is no coincidence, for example, that many fires burning in places like Yugoslavia and throughout the Mideast have been smoldering ever since the Holy Crusades.

Are the Present Times So Important?

As we have seen, the calendar year of Christ's birth (and hence the year two thousand) has no particular correlation to the millennium of Revelation or to any other prophecy, although many generations of scholars have tried to find some. Furthermore, the thousand-year mark on the calendar is an arbitrary decimal measure, originating with our ten-digit (ten-fingered) numbering system.

The millennium, however, has no connection to the durational cycles of nature. It has no mathematical relationship to any tick marks on the celestial clock. Astrology, which is based on astronomical cycles, would define a *new age*—into which the *Age of Aquarius* is currently dawning—as roughly twenty-one hundred years or slightly more than two millennia.

The most significant force that the millennium crossroad seems to have on society is this: The *collective expectations that people hold at these numerical milestones have triggered historically climactic events.* Let's step back in time to get some intriguing glimpses of these patterns.

Early Church Warnings

The generation immediately following Christ's lifetime was ripe with expectations of His Second Coming. We can sense the urgency in Paul's letters to the Christians in Thessalonica, a bustling seaport city in what is modern-day Greece. "Now, brothers, about the times and dates we do not need to write to you, for you know very well that the day of the Lord will come like a thief in the night . . . You are all sons of the light and sons of the day. So then, let us not be like others who are asleep, but let us be alert and self-controlled." Paul had to reassure them in a second letter that they had not missed the boat; "Concerning the coming of our Lord Jesus Christ and our being gathered to him, we ask you, brothers not to become easily unsettled or alarmed by some prophecy, report or letter supposedly to have come from us, saying that the day of the Lord has already come. Don't let anyone deceive you in any way, for that day will not come until the rebellion occurs and the man of lawlessness is revealed, the man doomed to destruction (1 Thessalonians 5:1–6 and 2 Thessalonians 2:1–3)."

From that time forward, even after the Zealot rebellion and fall of Jerusalem twenty years later, the feeling of immediate expectancy never dampened. The excitement that gripped subsequent generations of believers became a preoccupation for some. Many theories were offered, interpreting dates and events, often with complex mathematical calculations. It is fascinating to read about the various forms of appocalypticism and millenarianism appearing through history, and there are several good books on the subject by scholars of eschatology, including Norman Cohn's *The Pursuit of the Millennium;* and Damian Thompson's *The End of Time.* With them one can trace dozens of historical cases in which millennial expectations brought about enthusiasm for some, disappointment for others, and doom for many, but always in a different way than was predicted.

In A.D. 156, a heretic named Montanus proclaimed himself to be the Holy Spirit incarnate, and taught that the New Jerusalem of Revelation would physically descend from heaven onto the land of Phrygia (modern Turkey), very soon. He gathered such a following of believers that even when the phantom city didn't materialize, he sealed their loyalty with his own suicidal martyrdom. Instead of disbanding, Montanism spread farther and for a while even rivaled Christianity in far-flung regions from Rome to Africa. This may be the first recorded sect linking suicide with apocalyptic disappointment, foreshadowing the destiny of future cults, including Waco and many others.

In the third century, a highly regarded theologian named Origen denounced apocalyptic fever. He spoke of the coming Kingdom as a place that exists in the hearts of believers, that the struggles overcome in this life are rewarded in the afterlife. He was attempting to defuse the increasingly explosive apocalyptic and millenarian beliefs that were surfacing in worldly conflicts.

History shows another potential problem that can happen when separate cultures, each bristling with expectations, collide at the millennium. One such incident coincided with the one thousandth anniversary of Rome in A.D. 248. A special version of the Secular Games, forerunners of our Olympics, had just concluded its millennial tribute to the empire, which was suffering from a sagging national pride and a threatened traditional religion. The Emperor Decius, empowered by the furor of the celebrations, soon began the first systematic persecution of Christians across the empire. Those who refused to worship the Roman gods were tortured mercilessly. We are left to wonder if this was a coincidental clash at a millennial turning point, or a self-fulfilled expectation of something climactic. We don't know, but we do know that millennial thinking among Christians had become widespread by that time.

Millennial date watching took many zigzags. The variously innovative ways by which people arrived at certain end-time dates must have sounded reasonable to many in their own day. A rumor had circulated that St. Peter once struck a deal with Satan, and that the Church would survive only 365 years after the crucifixion. When an earthquake struck in A.D. 398, a panicked population went running to churches for baptism. In A.D. 410, panic again ensued after "Barbarians" took over Rome, triggering another speculation that the world had reached its six thousandth year since the creation, and would soon enter the millennium.

St. Augustine addressed those panics and the broader problem of end-time speculation. In Thompson's book, *The End of Time* we read, "The most conservative perspective of all was that of St. Augustine of Hippo, who ridiculed attempts to calculate the time of the end. 'In vain therefore do we try to reckon and set limits to the years that remain to this world, when we hear from the Mouth of Truth that it is not ours to know this. Yet some have said that four hundred, some five hundred, others even a thousand years must be reached between the Lord's ascension and his last coming.'" Augustine warned against falling into a panic over present happenings, "as if they were the ultimate and extreme of all things, so that we may not be laughed at by those who have read of more and worse things in the history of the world." St. Augustine, like Origen before him, was fighting the tide of millenarianism, which continually adapted itself to the calendar of the day.

Those soothing voices tried to bring spiritual stability and sanity to an otherwise chaotic world. Remember, these were the beginnings of the Dark Ages, a period when the likes of Atilla the Hun from the east and "Barbarians" from the north were raping and pillaging across Europe and would soon break the back of the Roman Empire. It probably felt like the end of time with every wave of foreign invasion, and there were numerous Antichrists, dark forces, and rumors of wars to spark apocalyptic beliefs that the world's days were numbered.

As we have found, there is not even one biblical reference indicating that a prophetic stopwatch began at the birth of Christ. In fact, the starting point of what we call Anno Domini (A.D.)—meaning "in the year of our Lord"—was only established five hundred and twenty-five years after Christ's birth. A monk named Dennis the Small was commissioned by Pope John I to replace the ancient Roman calendar. The old calendar had established its zero mark at the founding of Rome, seven hundred and fifty-three years before Christ. And there probably was a millennium-related reason for the Pope's request to readjust the calendar to a new reference point. The Church had already dealt with nearly four centuries of end-times speculations, confrontations, and disappointments among its followers, and was headed toward another crossroads at the end of the week—*the Great Week.*

A popular theory called "the Great Week" had taken hold, based on the idea of the seven days of Creation. It combined the one-week concept with a quote from St. Peter: "With the Lord a thousand years is like a day . . ." Figuring that the *millennial week* began at Creation, it was then calculated using biblical genealogy that the first *millennial day* of Creation began exactly five thousand five hundred years before Christ's birth. Therefore, if (according to Revelation) the Second Coming begins on the final *millennial day*, then the event would have to occur exactly six thousand years after Creation, on the five hundredth anniversary of Jesus' birth. In response to such logic, the Church had already averted the inevitable panic at the five-hundred-year mark by officially recalculating the Creation date to have been three hundred years later, conveniently pushing back the Second Coming until *eight hundred years* after Christ. Modern scholars think that the resetting of the calendar by Dennis the Small was another diversionary tactic, which would throw off the scent of millennial date chasers. That strategy would buy time, of course, only until A.D. 1000.

THE CRUSADES AND BEYOND

The world's stage was being set for a tragedy of truly apocalyptic proportions. In A.D. 623 a previously nomadic tribal society in Arabia was galvanized by a prophet named Mohammed, the founder of Islam. Through the written Koran, he prophesied a final Day of Judgment on which all people would be accountable for their lives, with rewards for those who worshiped God, and punishment for those who didn't. He also prophesied about a resurrection from the dead, lending a family resemblance to the prophecies from the other children of Abraham, the Hebrews and Christians. For Moslems, the battle between *good and evil* was primarily an inner struggle, but could sometimes manifest itself outwardly between people. Mohammed himself used military means when he thought it was necessary, firmly committed to preaching the Moslem Koran to godless pagans, even if by force. Above all, he stressed that the *Lord God is One.* He spoke warmly of Abraham, Moses, and Jesus, but advised that on certain issues concerning *God's Oneness*—particularly the idea of the Trinity—Moslems should respectfully correct believers from other religions. This kind of arguing was defined by Mohammed in the Islamic concept of *jihad:* "Therefore listen not to the unbelievers, but struggle against them with utmost strenuousness."

Meanwhile, Europe was thrashing about in the Dark Ages. Men's lives were consumed by indecisive wars that crisscrossed the continent. The Roman Church was extremely powerful, and for a while Europe was dubbed the *Holy Roman Empire.* Emperors and popes were closely linked and sometimes it was hard to know who held more power, politically and militarily.

The millennial year 1000 actually passed quite peacefully. Rather than an air of panic, there was a sense of exhilaration. Scholars point out that this kind of excitement often accompanies the first stage of millennium fever. In fact, a treaty called the "Peace of God" involved huge crowds gathering on fields in Limoges, where the warrior elite waved banners and swore oaths of pacifism. It was reportedly accompanied by mass healing as religious relics were given tribute. Interestingly, the emperor himself, Otto III, was deeply convinced they were in the final days, though the common people were not much stirred by the idea yet. An eyewitness report from A.D. 1003 describes a rebuilding boom of churches, monasteries, and chapels, "throughout the whole world, but especially in Italy and Gaul . . . rebuilt better than before." Although rumors circulated in later centuries about the *Terrors of 1000*, reports of mass suicides and widespread panic are unsupported, and are brushed off by serious historians as colorful myths. Actually, the average peasants probably didn't even know what date it was, nor would they have cared. The Church of Rome kept close reins on religious information and by that time had curtailed popular interest in millenarian sects. Still, many sermons and religious documents were written that referred to the Last Days, playing to the sense of doom and desperation that hung in the air after centuries of feudal warring and misery. For some, end-times anticipation provided a welcome relief and strengthened religious commitment. All signs of millennial enthusiasm were eventually overshadowed by the apocalyptic drama brewing behind the scenes, as we shall see.

The real millenarian dangers emerged a little while later, following the split between the Roman and Eastern Churches. By the millennial year 1000, the Church had been torn by a bitter feud between the *Roman Empire* and the Greek-speaking *Eastern Empire* (across from Serbia, in modern-day Turkey). Both were Christian empires, but the Eastern Christians didn't bow to the Roman pope. By the 1050s this split between *Roman Orthodox* and *Eastern Orthodox* churches became official, preparing the stage for the next dramatic act.

The Eastern Empire was being overrun by Islamic extremists who were about to take the Eastern Church's capital city of Constantinople. The East appealed to the Roman pope for reinforcements and the reply was well calculated. Here was a golden opportunity to achieve two ambitions: The pope could regain loyalty from the Eastern Empire; and at the same time could redirect the violence away from Europe's Franco-Germanic wars and toward the "dark forces" of Islam. Pope Urban II called for a religious war, a Holy Crusade, the War of the Cross.

Thus, the Holy Wars began, pitting two religiously fundamental fighting forces against each other. Every soul on either side, Christian or Islamic, believed that the other was the agent of Satan. Each was prepared to die while massacring countless innocent men, women, and children to regain Jerusalem on God's behalf. The atrocities committed by both sides are too numerous to list here. But for more than a hundred years, four separate Crusades swept from Europe to the Middle East splashing rivers of blood throughout the Holy Land. This was apocalyptic millenarianism at its worst. But it wasn't the final battle either.

Rather than reviewing an exhausting list of all the end-times episodes that followed from then until now—most smaller than the Crusades but just as devastating to those involved—let us look at a new millenarian pattern, begun by a religious philosopher from the twelfth century.

PATTERNS OF DECEPTION

An apocalyptic philosopher named Joachim of Fiore, during the time of the Crusades, devised a brilliantly complicated formula for calculating the future of mankind based on biblical prophecies but with a new twist. In essence, convinced that the current Middle East Crusades were the final battle that would usher Christ's return, he described how the world may soon enter the *third* age of civilization, the *Age of Spirit.* His tone was upbeat, and his implications inspired utopian fantasies for the millennium, creating whole new social structures. The devil was in the details, though, of how he tied together spiritual and political ambitions. Damian Thompson said about Joachim's influence, "Without necessarily meaning to, he had made the crucial connection between apocalyptic change and political reconstruction." In effect, his writings began a pattern of manipulative efforts to camouflage political strategies by first *defeating the Antichrist,* next bringing on an *earthly savior,* and finally entering into a *new golden era.* "The traces of Joachimite thinking in the writings of the popes, antipope critics, doomsday sects, Jesuits, English millenarian Protestants and French socialists are testimony to not only the power of his vision of the reformed godly society; they also illustrate the capacity of end-time ideas to mutate, so that different versions of an apocalyptic vision can be used simultaneously to bolster a political elite, to bring about a measured reform and to justify bloody revolution."

Thompson links many sobering scenarios that suggest that this new brand of millennial optimism laid the groundwork for the revolutionary patterns of recent centuries. One of the most chilling manifestations of Joachim's third age is the *Nazi Third Reich,* literally defined as the third stage of the Holy Roman Empire. Norman Cohn writes in *The Pursuit of the Millennium,* "the phrase 'the Third Reich' adopted as a name for that 'new order,' which was supposed to last a thousand years, would have had but little emotional significance if the fantasy of a third and most glorious dispensation had not, over the centuries, entered into the common stock of European social mythology." Thompson adds, "The Jews, for Hitler and his most fanatical followers, were a supernatural force for evil: and it was this conviction that made the Holocaust possible." The Third Reich mutated the millennialist paradigm, replacing biblical prophecies and trust in God with the pagan practice of consulting the ancient runes as a means of acquiring insight and power. The tendency to find the Antichrist in one's enemy was adapted by Hitler, for whom the Jewish people became the epitome of evil. During its reign, the Third Reich itself was accused by many as personifying the Antichrist, and with its loveless message, the Nazi philosophy reverted to a style of barbarism more horrifying than anything faced by the ancient Jews.

༄

Today, if we are to take responsibility for our own words and deeds, then we must learn from our ancestors and not project the devil's mask onto other human beings. The generation of the year 2000, and ones that follow, will be accountable to human history for its wise, or unwise, handling of the knowledge of its past. We can learn profound lessons from the written archives that recount the millennial bridges people have crossed and survived, sometimes just barely.

One week after the Bomb was dropped on Japan, James Agee wrote in *Time* magazine: "The promise of good and of evil bordered alike on the infinite . . . When the bomb split open the universe and revealed the prospect of the infinitely extraordinary, it also revealed the oldest, simplest, commonest, most neglected and most important of facts: that each man is *eternally and above all else responsible for his own soul*, and, in the terrible words of the Psalmist, that no man may deliver his brother, nor make agreement unto God for him. Man's fate has forever been shaped between the hands of reason and spirit, now in collaboration, again in conflict. Now *reason* and *spirit* meet on final ground. If either or anything is to survive, they must find a way to create an indissoluble partnership."

Finding the bridge between reason and spirit is exactly the challenge we find in our path at this time. Agee's nearly prophetic—and apocalyptic—appeal to his own generation more than a half-century ago needs to be remembered and impressed on our subconscious. For we are, at this millennial checkpoint, entering a volatile moment in history and, as George Ritchie's near-death vision of the future reflected, we are individually responsible for our own soul and the energies at our command.

CHAPTER 23

Final Reflections

As water reflects a face,
so a man's heart reflects the man.
—PROVERBS 27:19

HAT DIFFERENCE does it make if people spend their time anticipating the end of the world, anyway?" one might ask. "So what if Chicken Little wants to crow that the sky is falling?" Isn't the genuine concern for the well-being of others worth risking an embarrassment of a possible false alarm? After all, using the *fear of God* to help straighten people out never hurts, right?

If getting people agitated in this way is so harmless, then why did Jesus, Paul, and Augustine advise people not to set their sights on the end times? Paul's advice "not to become easily unsettled or alarmed" was a call to avoid deceptions and to remain focused on spiritual steadfastness. But in spite of the sage advice, people historically tended to preach getting right with God *because* the end is near! Doing so draws attention to worldly fears and away from spiritual issues. What happens to one's belief in the event of a no-show? Many appointments have been broken, and with them many hearts and faiths. And it is in the wake of such disappointments that various fringe groups tend to emerge, bent on *helping to bring on the final conflict* . . .

1420—Bohemia: Christ is scheduled to arrive on February 14, accompanied by fire. The only towns foretold to survive are in the Taborite Mountains. Followers give all their money to Taborite priests. When the deadline passes, their initial pacifism turns to vengeance, and followers go on a killing spree. One faction, advocating free sex and mass murder, turns on a rival faction and is entirely wiped out.

1534—Germany: Munster is overrun by an apocalyptic sect, isolating itself militarily. Puritanism gives way to sexual abandon, one madman replaces another and appoints himself Messiah. Mass starvation and public beheadings precede the town's liberation and the execution of all leaders.

1650—England: Millenarianism sweeps through British society, where the date of the end ranges from 1651 to 1700. Many prophets emerge, and one millenarian group nearly overtakes Parliament. The movement evolves into a militia, staging a bloody clash with British guards. Its leader, who claims to be Christ incarnate, is executed for treason.

1843—United States: Christ's return is calculated by a New York farmer who is "fully convinced that sometime between March 21, 1843, and March 21, 1844, Christ will come and bring all his saints with him." Mass publicity draws large followings, between fifty thousand and a million, ranging in degrees of conviction. *The Great Disappointment* follows the missed date, and followers are taunted, "What, not gone up yet? We thought you'd gone up! Wife didn't leave you to burn, did she?"

20th Century—Worldwide: Millenarian movements evolve into mainstream religions of Jehovah's Witnesses, Seventh-Day Adventists, and Mormons. Smaller offshoots and other millenarian groups constitute fringe cults that make the news: Waco's *Branch Davidians* die in fiery blaze; Japan's *Aum Shinrikyo* launch sarin gas attack in Tokyo's subways; Jonestown's *People's Temple* commit mass suicide with cyanide-laced Kool-Aid; Islamic *jihad terrorists* bomb the World Trade Center, airlines, embassies, etc.; Switzerland's *Order of the Solar Temple* commit mass suicide and murder; San Diego's *Heaven's Gate* cult commit mass suicide to "beam-up to a spaceship" in a comet's tail . . .

꩜

If all of this millennial talk seems a bit abstract, where religious doctrines are whirling together with textbook stories from past and current events, then perhaps the following real-life story will help to bring it home.

While talking with a close friend about the study I was doing on *end-time* trends, she revealed her own family's experience in the wake of millenarian disappointment.

HITTING HOME

In the winter of 1988, Diana, a young expectant mother, was busy making her holiday plans. Christmas was her favorite season. She loved the music, the decorations, and the smell of holiday feasts. Most of all, though, Diana cherished the promise of love, joy, and peace on earth. After all, wasn't that the real reason Jesus had been born, to teach us how to truly love one another? Diana hung her Christmas lights, singing softly to herself, "Oh, tidings of comfort and joy . . ." Just then, she heard the mail truck rattle by.

Heading into the bright sunshine that day to retrieve the mail, Diana was unaware that she was about to receive tidings of a different kind—a letter from her sister-in-law, Shirley. In it, Shirley told how she and her husband had attended a church service the previous night. The speaker that evening was the author of a book that predicted when the Second Coming would occur. Both Shirley and Diana's brother, Bruce, had been convinced that the end of the world was near. "In fact," Shirley cautioned, "it will end in the next few weeks."

Diana stared at the words in disbelief. She couldn't help but wonder, *Have my brother and his wife lost their minds?* Taking a deep breath, she continued reading. The letter warned her to "get her life right." Several years earlier, Diana had converted from Southern Baptist to Catholicism when she married a Catholic man. Now, Shirley urged Diana to "repent and become saved," thus allowing them all to be together when the Rapture occurred. Shirley further explained that she and her husband had already made arrangements to leave their car keys, money, and even the *deed to their house* to some Jewish acquaintances, "who, of course, would not be raptured." Included with the letter were several tapes by the author of the book for Diana to listen to.

Diana tossed the tapes to one side. She didn't need to listen to them. As far as she was concerned, this was all nonsense. What she really needed right now was someone sane to talk to. She called her parents' home. Her mother answered. "Mom," Diana started in immediately, "you won't believe this crazy letter I just got from Shirley." Diana sensed a certain air of quietness in her mother, but dismissing it, continued on with her story. Finally, her mother responded, "Your father and I also went to that church service. We believe it, too." Diana was stunned. She asked to speak with her father. He was the son of a preacher—she had *heard him* quote the Bible verse that says *"no man will know the day or hour."* Surely *he* couldn't have fallen for all of this. Diana's father explained that although he wasn't totally convinced, it did make "a lot of sense to him in a mathematical sort of way."

And so, along with her parents' good-byes were more warnings to "listen to the tapes and get right with God." Tears filled Diana's eyes as she hung up the phone. But she still had one last hope for a voice of reason. Her grandparents. They were strong Christians and she had always trusted their judgment. She called them, expecting words of encouragement. Within moments of their conversation, however, Diana realized that they, too, had heard the tapes and were somewhat if not fully convinced. Diana found herself wondering, *How could Grandfather believe that the end of the world was actually just two weeks away?* A feeling of complete loneliness swept over her as she hung up the phone. Here she was, a woman expecting her first child soon. She should be happy. Instead, she found herself feeling absolutely alienated from the people she loved and needed most.

Later that night, Diana's husband, Rusty, returned from work. As Diana filled him in on the end-of-the-world prophesy, Rusty's temper flared. He phoned Shirley immediately. A heated argument ensued as Rusty proceeded to tell her "exactly what he thought of her 'Rapture.'" Not one to back down, Shirley was quick to remind him "where he was going." Diana remembers that moment well. "I knew things would never be the same between my family and me."

Several weeks went by and the big day loomed before them. Although Diana did not believe the world would end, she often found herself wondering about her family. *When the day comes and goes, will we ever talk about this again?*

Finally the day arrived. Diana got up as usual, went to work, and later that night, came home. The world had not ended. Neither her family, nor anyone else, had been raptured. Life simply went on. No one said a word about the event, or lack thereof. And because she didn't want to say *"I told you so,"* Diana didn't bring up the subject either.

But somewhere deep inside, Diana secretly hoped that someday her family would apologize for being misled and how it caused them to judge her so severely. She could admit that, in the heat of the moment, they probably had her best interests at heart. But couldn't they also see how much they had hurt her with their critical and judgmental assaults on her chosen faith? This *emotional* wedge that separated Diana from her family remained unresolved for more than ten years. And the chasm of alienation widened still further when her marriage ended, leaving her as a single mother to raise her daughter by herself.

Diana continued to live the life that she felt God wanted her to lead. She devoted her time to serving others as a maternity nurse, and then as a massage therapist. She got involved with prison ministry and visiting the elderly in nursing homes. She also developed a fascination for angels. Diana enjoyed reading about them and found much spiritual comfort in the messages brought to people who had actually experienced divine encounters. She prayed constantly and, within her own framework of traditional religion and real-life experience, enjoyed a confident and personal faith in God. By the time my wife and I first met Diana several years ago, she exhibited one of the most loving and Christlike attitudes of anyone we knew. Her family connections had gradually been reestablished, largely due to their mutual love for Diana's daughter.

Recently, after telling us about the experience with her family's end-times incident, Diana did something which I think was brave. She phoned her mom and dad especially to talk about the old wounds caused by their affront to her beliefs. Apparently, they had never realized just how deeply Diana had been hurt by their zealous, but temporary, fervor about the end of the world.

In the meantime, the family had changed its attitudes about trying to predict the future. Her mom had long since thrown the books out. And her dad realized that in their zeal to save their daughter's soul, they had overlooked her *feelings*. He had also decided it was best not to judge others. He and Diana even joked that God probably has *separate rooms* in Heaven for Baptists and Catholics.

Diana is grateful for the healing that has taken place between her and her family. She has seen firsthand how God is working in all their hearts, using His love and forgiveness to heal the wounds of misunderstanding.

❧

So, just where is this supposed millennial battleground? Is it valid to wait in suspense for a worldly battle—or a heavenly Kingdom—when even Jesus said, "the kingdom of God *is within you.*" Waiting for the final battle to come outwardly takes one's attention away from where the struggle is really staged—*in the heart* of every living man, woman, and child on Earth. The war between light and darkness is not relegated to be fought between countries, ethnic groups, or religious factions, but is a fight waged within each of us, every day. The internal struggle—between the positive and negative inner voices that offer us choices ten thousand times a day—is won or lost, moment by moment, on an individual basis. We choose to be on the winning side, in the light, when we exert our free will to obey the *still, small voice,* and tell the negative one *where to go.*

If Christ was, in fact, the fulfillment of the messianic prophecy of Isaiah, "a *light* for the Gentiles, to open eyes that are blind, to free captives from prison and to release from the dungeon those who sit in *darkness,*" then the final battle against darkness has already been won. We wouldn't have to wait any longer for some outward conquest. He would have accomplished it already by His Resurrection. It demonstrated His power over death, opening peoples' eyes to an eternal lighthouse and guiding those lost in darkness, on earth and elsewhere. All that would remain is for each of us to choose where we want to be, in the light or in the dark.

I believe that without having known it at the time, this is exactly what happened to me when I asked Christ to reveal Himself to me. I willingly chose to open my heart to the light of His love. I also believe that those whose near-death experiences have taken them beyond the earthly perspective have glimpsed that pure light. And through that light, if we choose to enter, we are drawn into an eternal spiritual realm, like through some sort of doorway.

THE LIGHT IS LOVE

Jesus told his disciples,
"As the Father has loved me, so have I loved you.
Now remain in my love.
If you obey my commands,
you will remain in my love,
just as I have obeyed my Father's commands
and remain in his love . . ."

—JOHN 15:9–10

Everybody, in every generation, encounters certain crossroads where they must make choices of their own free will. We all are faced with decisions concerning our priorities: how we spend our time; whether to chase material success, social status, physical pleasures, and other *things*, or, instead, to pursue spiritual peace, self-control, and other heartfelt understandings of ancient wisdom, especially the importance of *love for others*. Choosing *to be in the light* and choosing *to love others* are eternally inseparable ideas.

I believe the quest to find one's purpose in life is taken by everyone, although every single one of us takes a uniquely different route. As original as snowflakes, no two lives have ever been the same nor have they been faced with exactly the same decisions along their life paths. Each of us journeys down the same highway, passing similar signs. But each takes a different combination of exits, detours, rest stops, and refueling choices. I myself have taken some detours in my past that have delayed my progress. At times I have been prone to take unwise risks along dangerous stretches in life, and have had my share of accidents. At other stages of my quest I have relaxed a bit too long in the kind of empty religious hypocrisy that Jesus warned about. I tried to shortcut the nitty-gritty goals of loving God and loving other people by instead filling my time and thoughts with doctrinal hairsplitting, lending too much importance to one particular religious group or another. Another, almost hypnotizing and numbing concern along the way has been the basic day-to-day task of keeping gas in my car and food in my belly. Ironically, the concern with *making a living* can, like some strange mirror trick, replace the challenge of *making a life*.

There is a divinely inspired section of one of Paul's letters that has been labeled *"the Love Chapter."* It sums up for me the entire message of Christ's Great Commandment: to love God and love one another. Every time I read this beautiful piece of writing, I find that each word has expanded in my life and takes a deeper meaning:

> *If I speak in the tongues of men and of angels, but have not love, I am only a resounding gong or a clanging cymbal. If I have the gift of prophecy and can*

fathom all mysteries and all knowledge, and if I have a faith that can move mountains, but have not love I am nothing. If I give all I possess to the poor and surrender my body to the flames, but have not love, I gain nothing.

Love is patient, love is kind. It does not envy, it does not boast, it is not proud. It is not rude, it is not self-seeking, it is not easily angered, it keeps no record of wrongs. Love does not delight in evil but rejoices with the truth. It always protects, always trusts, always hopes, always perseveres.

Love never fails. But where there are prophecies, they will cease; where there are tongues, they will be stilled; where there is knowledge, it will pass away. For we know in part and we prophesy in part, but when perfection comes, the imperfect disappears. When I was a child, I talked like a child, I thought like a child, I reasoned like a child. When I became a man, I put childish ways behind me. Now we see but a poor reflection as in a mirror; Then we shall see face to face. Now I know in part; then I shall know fully, even as I am fully known.

And now these three remain: faith, hope and love. But the greatest of these is love.

—1 CORINTHIANS 13:1–13

∾

I am blessed to have a family that reminds me constantly of *God's love for us.* From the oldest to the young est members, they all are sharing God's love through the *love that they have for one another.*

The other night, my little girl asked a question that reminded me about life's great design. I was reading her a bedtime story like I do every night. It was a beautiful book from the library called *A Time for Everything,* which combines verses from Ecclesiastes together with old paintings from many different cultures to illustrate each idea:

There is a time for everything,
and a season for every purpose under heaven:
a time to be born and a time to die,
a time to plant and a time to uproot,
a time to kill and a time to heal,
a time to tear down and a time to build,
a time to weep and a time to laugh,
a time to mourn and a time to dance,
a time to scatter stones and a time to gather stones together,
a time to embrace and a time to refrain from embracing,
a time to search and a time to give up,
a time to keep and a time to throw away,
a time to tear and a time to mend,
a time to be silent and a time to speak,
a time to love and a time to hate,
a time for war and a time for peace.
　　　　　　　　　　　　—ECCLESIASTES 3:1–8

When I finished reading, Christina gently asked, "Papa, what is *war?*"

Oh, God, she's three and a half years old . . . How do I begin to answer a question like that?

"Well," I said, "it's a sad time when people fight against other people. It's a very sad time."

Christina waited, probably reflecting on the little fights she's had with her sister, Grace—and softly agreed, "Yes, it is . . ."

And I realized, at that moment, that we really are here for a wonderful purpose. I pray I am given enough days to try addressing all of the questions that will certainly come;

about death and life,
about fear and love,
about pain and forgiveness,
about sadness and real joy,
about loving other people and loving God,
and about the Lord's never ending love for us . . .

Thank You, Father, for whatever time You give to pass on the things You have shown us to these sweet and bright-spirited children of Yours. Please guide and protect them, and all future generations of seekers. Let us reflect Your compassion through our lives, and help us to lovingly point to Your *Kingdom of Heaven,* which You have created in our hearts. *Please, Father, let it be.*

Appendix: Scriptural Keys to the Kingdom of Heaven & the Light

"The true light *that gives light to every man was coming into the world.*"

—JOHN 1:9

"In him was life, and that life was the light of men. The light shines in the darkness, but the darkness has not understood it." —JOHN 1:4–5

"The Christ would suffer and, as the first to rise from the dead, would proclaim light to his own people and to the Gentiles." —ACTS 26:23

Jesus said, "I am the light of the world. Whoever follows me will never walk in darkness, but will have the light of life." —JOHN 8:12

"The people living in darkness have seen a great light; on those living in the land of the shadow of death a light has dawned." —MATTHEW 4:16

"Joyfully [give] thanks to the Father, who has qualified you to share in the inheritance of the saints in the kingdom of light. *For he has rescued us from the dominion of darkness and brought us into the kingdom of the Son he loves, in whom we have redemption, the forgiveness of sins.*" —COLOSSIANS 1:12–14

"You are all sons of the light, and sons of the day."—1 THESSALONIANS 5:5

"The darkness is passing, and the true light is already shining. Anyone who claims to be in the light but hates his brother is still in darkness. Whoever loves his brother lives in the light."   —1 JOHN 2:8–9

"But you are a chosen people . . . that you may declare the praises of him who called you out of darkness into his wonderful light."   —1 PETER 2:9

"You are the light of the world. A city on a hill cannot be hidden. Neither do people put a lamp under a bowl. Instead they put it on its stand and it gives light to everyone in the house. In the same way let your light shine before men, that they may see your good deeds, and praise your Father in heaven."   —MATTHEW 5:14–16

"For God, who said, 'Let light shine out of darkness,' made his light shine in our hearts to give us the light of the knowledge of the glory of God in the face of Christ."   —2 CORINTHIANS 4:6

"The light of the righteous shines brightly, but the lamp of the wicked is snuffed out."   —PROVERBS 13:9

"The Lord is my light and my salvation."   —PSALM 27:1

"As long as it is day, we must do the work of him who sent me. Night is coming, when no one can work. While I am in the world, I am the light of the world."   —JOHN 9:4–5

Resources and Recommended Reading:

Out of the Silence. Duane Miller. Nashville, TN: Thomas Nelson Inc., 1996. (By the man who lost his voice in "At a Loss for Words.") Visit Duane's Web site at www.nuvoice.org or e-mail Duane at: nuvoice@nuvoice.org.

God's Got Your Number. Ken Gaub. Green Forest, AR: New Leaf Press, 1986. (By the man who received the person to person call in "Heaven Calling.")

Dreams, Plans, and Goals. Ken Gaub. Green Forest, AR: New Leaf Press, 1998. For information on Ken Gaub's ministries and speaking engagements or to order his books, write to him at P.O. Box 1, Yakima, WA 98907 or visit his Web site at: www.kengaub.com.

Where Miracles Happen. Joan Wester Anderson. New York: Ballantine Books, 1994.

Where Angels Walk. Joan Wester Anderson. New York: Ballantine Books, 1992.

An Angel to Watch Over Me. Joan Wester Anderson. New York: Ballantine Books, 1994.

The Power of Miracles. Joan Wester Anderson. New York: Ballantine Books, 1998.

Celebration of Miracles. Jodie Berndt. Nashville, TN: Thomas Nelson Inc., 1995.

Celebration of Angels. Timothy Jones. Nashville, TN: Thomas Nelson Inc., 1994.

The Art of Prayer. Timothy Jones. New York: Ballantine Books, 1997.

Do You Have a Guardian Angel? John Ronner. Murfreesboro, TN: Mamre Press, 1985. P.O. Box 3137, Murfreesboro, TN 37133 / e-mail: mamrepress@aol.com.

Know Your Angels. John Ronner. Murfreesboro, TN: Mamre Press. P.O. Box 3137, Murfreesboro, TN 37133 / e-mail: mamrepress@aol.com.

A Book of Angels. Sophy Burnham. New York: Ballantine Books, 1990.

Life After Life. Dr. Raymond A. Moody. New York: Mockingbird/Bantam, 1975.

Reflections on Life After Life. Dr. Raymond A. Moody. New York: Mockingbird/Bantam, 1977.

The Light Beyond. Dr. Raymond A. Moody. New York: Bantam, 1988.

Lessons from the Light. Sandra Rogers. New York: Warner Books, 1995.

Ordered to Return: My Life After Dying. Dr. George Ritchie. Charlottesville, VA: Hampton Roads Publishing, 1998.

Return from Tomorrow. Dr. George Ritchie. Fleming H. Revell Co., 1988.

Embraced by the Light. Betty J. Eadie. Placerville, CA: Gold Leaf Press, 1992.

Transformed by the Light. Melvin Morse, M.D. New York: Villard Books, 1992.

Saved by the Light. Dannion Brinkley. New York: Villard Books, 1994.

Incredible Coincidence. Alan Vaughan. New York: Ballantine Books, 1979.

Every Day's a Miracle. Paul Robert Walker. New York: Avon Books, 1995.

The Pursuit of the Millennium. Norman Cohn. New York: Oxford University Press, 1970.

The End of Time. Damian Thompson. Hanover and London: University Press of New England, 1996.

A Short History of the World. H. G. Wells. New York: Macmillan, 1922.

The First Century. William K. Klingaman. New York: Harper Perennial, 1986.

Peter Shockey's videos can be obtained from the following vendors:
Internet orders at: **http://www.amazon.com** (Search: Videos by title)

Life After Life; *Based on the bestselling book by Dr. Raymond Moody, this New York Film Festival Award-winning film unravels the mysteries surrounding the experience of dying. The author introduces six of his most compelling cases, each telling their own fascinating story of their brush with death—and beyond. Brilliant special effects accompany this sensitive study of a universally shared, and greatly misunderstood topic.* One tape: 57 minutes NTSC

Angel Stories; *Parts 1&2. Continuing the supernatural portrayals of angelic beings which are a common element in the near-death experience, this two-part special investigates twenty different stories in which people claim to have encountered angelic beings who brought important messages, healing and heroic rescue in times of need. Authors and experts share their views on contemporary and historical angel sightings.* Two tapes: 47 minutes ea. NTSC

Miracles Are Real; *Parts 1&2 or Abridged. Following the popular interest in angels came a subsequent wave of stories about miraculous phenomena which were often attributed to angelic influence or divine intervention. This two-part special presents twenty amazing incidents in which real people describe their often death-defying, sometimes unbelievable "coincidences" which were frequently felt to be answers to prayer.* Available as Boxed Set of 1&2, or 80 minutes abridged version NTSC

Angel Chants; *Gift video. Magnificent paintings of angels from throughout art history are choreographed to a contemporary musical score, composed and performed by Peter's wife, Stowe Dailey Shockey. This video was completed exactly one week before their daughter Christina Leigh Shockey was conceived.* 30 minutes NTSC

Heaven Sent; Includes *Miracles Are Real (abridged)* and *Angels with Us. These stories, many in our time, involve miraculous healings, supernatural rescues, and angelic messages sent in time of great need. Included is the angel visitation experienced by famous*

Hollywood actor Mickey Rooney and the lifesaving angelic visit at Abraham Lincoln's birth. 2 tape Boxed Set NTSC

Or at:

PBS Videos: You can order videos twenty-four hours a day, seven days a week by Internet, phone, fax, or mail with your credit card.

- http://shop.pbs.org (Search: Alphabetical list)
- Phone: 800-645-4PBS
- Fax: 703-739-8131
- Or you can mail your order to PBS Home Video, P.O. Box 751089, Charlotte, NC 28275. Be sure to include the item title and number.

Life After Life: A1506-WEBHV

Angel Stories: A1629-WEBHV

Miracles Are Real: A2426-WEBHV

Or at:

Miracles and Heavenly Visions: 1-800-380-2357